COUNTRY OF THE SPIRIT...
VATICAN CITY

Country of the Spirit...

VATICAN CITY

FRANK J. KORN

ST. PAUL EDITIONS

NIHIL OBSTAT:
  Rev. Richard V. Lawlor, S.J.

IMPRIMATUR:
  ✠ Humberto Cardinal Medeiros
  Archbishop of Boston

Library of Congress Cataloging in Publication Data

Korn, Frank J.
  Country of the Spirit, Vatican City.

  1. Vatican City—Description—Guide-books. I. Title.
DG792.K67   914.5'63404928   81-19567
                                    AACR2

ISBN 0-8198-1415-6 (cloth)
      0-8198-1416-4 (paper)

Printed in the U.S.A. by the Daughters of St. Paul
50 St. Paul's Ave., Boston, MA 02130

The Daughters of St. Paul are an international congregation of religious women serving the Church with the
communications media.

83-4437

DEDICATION

With all paternal love to
Frank, Ronald and John

—FJK

ACKNOWLEDGEMENTS

With profound gratitude to
—my wife, Camille, for all her typing and suggestions.
—my former student, JoAnn Cavallo, for her proof-
reading and encouragement.
—my dear friend Aldo Miralli, for introducing me to the
fascinating world of the Vatican.

—FJK

Contents

Foreword

March 1, 1965: an obscure date perhaps for everyone else, but for me it was the turning point of my life. I still remember that fateful day when walking through Sant'Anna's Gate, almost timidly, I set foot in the Vatican, on my way to officially become a member of the *Gendarmeria Pontificia* (security bureau of the Vatican). It was a warm, radiant morning, the air already filled with the captivating scent of the imminent spring. I recall how the Swiss guard on duty at the gate gently approached me (to my surprise he spoke my language) asking where I was going; and how I stood in awe in front of him, nearly speechless, admiring his artistically designed blue uniform. Thus began my life in that tiny, seemingly magic world, Vatican City, of which I was a citizen and full-time resident until the end of 1970 when, in the wake of a series of internal reforms, Pope Paul VI dissolved the Gendarmeria Pontificia—a military corps—and created in its stead a civilian organization. On January 20, 1971, the newly formed body assumed the official name of *Ufficio Centrale di Vigilanza* (roughly, Central Bureau of Vigilance) of which I was a member until 1976, the year I left the Vatican to come to America where I took up residence.

I feel obliged to the author for having given me the opportunity to bring back fond memories. It is, in fact, with profound joy that I set about to write these lines, not only because they deal with Vatican City, but also because they concern a period of my life which I cherish.

Frank Korn's splendid work is the spontaneous result of his deep and genuine love of history; endowed with the adventurous spirit of a true explorer, he is in constant search of the truth, the desire to learn and deepen the extent of his knowledge ever present in him. His style is smooth, flowing; his approach gentle, yet vigorous and vibrant.

True, Korn deals here with perhaps one of the most celebrated places on earth; yet, just as no two persons are equal, so am I firmly convinced that no two writers' treatment of the same subject will ever be alike: each has his own distinctive personality, perspective, and style. The author's main purpose throughout the book is to highlight the characteristics of the Vatican as a country and the role of the Pontiff as head of state as well as the spiritual leader of the Church; for Vatican City is, yes, the pulsating heart of the Catholic community but it is also the headquarters of a complex, yet marvelously arranged, network of diplomatic ties spreading virtually all over the world.

Upon reading the manuscript I was, from time to time, overtaken by the "sweet" pangs of nostalgia, the power of Korn's words—through his accurate description of certain events of which I myself was at times either a witness or a protagonist—at some points evoking images and provoking emotions that gave me, for long moments, the illusion of being back in Vatican City, or at Castel Gandolfo, the summer residence of the Popes.

For example, because of his numerous ties within the Vatican walls, but more importantly by virtue of his acute sense of observation, the author has been able to draw a detailed and quite interesting account of one of John Paul II's typically routine days. The reader will ideally be taken by the hand and will be led, as an invisible guest at the side of the reigning Pope, through the various rooms of the Apostolic Palace, sharing in the Pope's long and laborious day. The author has also captured the unforgettable moments of John Paul II's visit to Yankee Stadium on October 2, 1979. Korn was there, and reading the touching description he gave of that event will be as memorable for the reader as if he had been there too.

Vatican City: a minute country with myriads of organizations, a small territory where extremely important decisions are made every day; decisions at times powerful enough to affect the lives, one way or another, of some 750 million Catholics scattered in all the continents. Enriched with moving anecdotes and some of the author's personal experiences in the Eternal City, this book will, in my opinion, help to penetrate the air of mystery that for many people still surrounds the Vatican, true lighthouse in the eternal ocean of Christendom.

Giancarlo Tonelli
Member — Vatican Vigilanza
1965-1976

Introduction

Vatican City
Summer, A.D. 1981

We believe, my wife and I, that our three young sons have an unusually deep and fervent Catholic Faith, particularly noteworthy in these troubled days, days of shrinking church attendance and rising hedonism, of dwindling vocations and soaring immorality. Our era is one in which it is simply not chic—especially for the young—to be a practicing and obedient son or daughter of Mother Church and Her Supreme Pontiff.

But then our sons, because of our summer residence in the Apostolic City, have had some unusual spiritual advantages. Countless times they have been to the Vatican to see and be blessed by the Holy Father; countless times, too, they have roamed the Papal burial grottoes beneath St. Peter's Basilica, offering prayers at the tomb of Peter and of so many of his successors; and countless other times they have accompanied me in my work as a guide to the Chapel of the Popes in the Catacombs of St. Callistus.

Here on Vatican Hill they have learned *in situ* of the birth, growth, and Divine Mandate of the Papal Office. Here they have come to know of the sanctity and greatness and martyrdom of Peter and many later bishops of Rome. Here they have come to stand in reverence and awe of the eternal strength of the institutional Church and the Papacy, in the face of twenty centuries of constant and violent attacks upon them both.

19

In the fateful summer of A.D. 1963 John Kennedy went to Berlin and viewed the 'Wall of Shame.' Throughout his great *Ich Bin Ein Berliner* speech on that occasion, he exhorted those who were apathetic toward the perils of communism with the ringing phrase: "Let them come to Berlin!"

And so with respect to those Catholics by birth who have lost or forsaken their religion I say: "Let them come to Rome!"

Regarding those unfortunates who naively believe all the slander that has been written and spoken for two millennia about the Church I say too: "Let them come to Rome!"

For those who know little or nothing about the Chair of Peter, but are eager to learn, I say as well: "Let them come to Rome!"

Let them come here and walk among the tombs and shrines of our spiritual forebears. Let them come here where untold thousands of early Christians nurtured the Seed of the Faith with their own blood. Let them come to the City of Peter and dare to go away without a reverence and admiration and indebtedness for the first Holy Father and for the vast majority of those who followed him to the Pontifical chair. (The fact that a few of them showed themselves wholly unfit for the Vicarship of Christ serves only to underscore that Christ intended His Church to be human as well as divine.)

Having walked almost in the footsteps of Peter here in this historic city, and having had his successor practically as their very own parish priest, our sons now have a grasp of and love for the Papacy which will contribute enormously to their spiritual growth and religious stability for the rest of their lives. Awaiting all visitors—especially Catholics—who come here, to the far bank of the Tiber, is the same priceless opportunity.

"Let them come to Rome. Let them come to the Vatican!"

But if you cannot come to the Vatican perhaps you can find the time to read my humble book on this most remarkable of places.

And why should anyone in the first place be interested in the subject at all?

Because the Vatican is a country, a most unusual, fascinating country. And it houses a government that was functioning in the days of Tiberius' Rome and is still functioning today, the government of the universal, apostolic, Catholic Church. Today's Vatican is organized very much along the lines of other modern governments with cabinets, departments, commissions, judicial courts, treasury, and whatever is necessary to operate efficiently a vast and complex organization.

The Vatican has been the residence of the Popes for about six centuries (since 1377). Before the transfer of the Pontifical Court to Avignon in the south of France (1309-1377) the Papal See was at the Lateran. But the territory of the Vatican has had a significant role in the history of the Church even from the days of Peter. And for twenty centuries the history of the Vatican has been the history of the world. The world has turned over many times since Christ made Peter His personal Vicar on Earth. Wars beyond number have raged, empires by the score have tumbled, civilizations have disappeared without a trace, a continent has even sunk into the sea since Peter was martyred on Vatican Hill. All these things have passed away but the Vatican and its government still remain. The Papacy lives on. The Chair of Peter is still occupied. Its occupant reigns over a baptized constituency of three-quarters of a billion persons living in all corners of the globe nearly twenty centuries after the crucifixion of Christ.

And why should anyone be the least bit interested in what I have to say on the matter?

Stendhal in the foreword to his Roman Journal pointed out that he had been to Rome six times. "I venture to recall this small circumstance," he wrote, "because it will perhaps incline the reader to vouchsafe me a measure of his confidence."

I have lived, studied, written, and taught in Rome on and off for over a decade now. All these endeavors have brought me into and out of the Vatican hundreds of times. And, like Stendhal, I point this out only so that you might vouchsafe me a measure of your confidence in my knowledge of the subject matter treated herein.

At the outset I shall promise not to be encyclopedic in style. For there are volumes by the score so written on this topic. My feeling is that one's appreciation of the Vatican and the Papacy need not be weighted down by too much erudition. In my volume I shall strive for readability. More than that I shall try almost to speak to you, as though I were sitting in your den or living room or out on your front porch, in a conversational simplicity on a subject in which you presumably are interested and with which I profess to have some familiarity.

Thank you for inviting me.

—Frank J. Korn

The Vatican City-State

Crossing the Tiber to St. Peter's and the Vatican via the Ponte Vittorio Emanuele, one is soon treated to a magnificent sight: the soaring, dazzling white marble, Michelangelesque dome of the largest Church in Christendom, outlined starkly against the limpid blue Roman sky. Once inside the Basilica of St. Peter, one sees, encircling the base of the cupola, in Latin letters seven feet tall, the declaration by Christ that inaugurated the holy and immortal institution of Mother Church and its concomitant institution, the Papacy: TU ES PETRUS ET SUPER HANC PETRAM AEDIFICABO ECCLESIAM MEAM ET TIBI DABO CLAVES REGNI CAELORUM. (Thou art Peter and upon this Rock I shall build my Church and I shall give unto you the Keys of the Kingdom of Heaven.)

Just as the dome of the Capitol in Washington is a cherished symbol to every American of our great democracy, the dome of St. Peter's is a cherished symbol to every Catholic, everywhere, of his or her citizenship in a very special country, a country of the spirit.

While Christ's Kingdom is not of this world, His Church is, at least in part. Therefore like any other institution, the Church is in need of property from which to conduct Her business with the world. Within the ancient city of Rome is a parcel of land which serves as the site of the terrestrial headquarters of the Universal

Church. This chapter will concern itself with the history, current status, and landmarks of that tiny territory.

As you step into St. Peter's Square and the shadow of the greatest temple in all of Christendom, the whole breathtaking panorama of Papal history stretches out before you. For this is the Vatican, site of Peter's murder and burial, of medieval pageantry and politics, of Renaissance and Baroque masterpieces, of Papal resistance to the *Risorgimento,* of political asylum for the persecuted Jews of World War II, of the home of the Supreme Pontiffs for the last seven centuries. It is the smallest country in the world with respect to geography (108 acres), yet the largest—by far—with respect to constituency (more than 750 million Catholics dispersed around the globe).

Bounded by the city of Rome on every side, this "country of the spirit" is fortified by the soaring honey-colored walls put up by Leo IV in the middle of the ninth century and for this reason enjoys, with some history-minded people, the nickname of the "Leonine City."

In St. Peter's day this hilly area north of the Tiber was known as *Ager Vaticanus* (the Vatican meadows). In the time of Julius Caesar it was just beginning to be developed. Some patricians had private villas there, and there were public gardens with monuments to Romulus, Numa Pompilius, Caesar himself, and other luminaries of Roman history. On the western slope the deranged Caligula built a *circus,* i.e., a chariot racetrack where during the reign of the bestial Nero massive executions of Christians often took place.

According to Christian tradition the Apostolic Prince, Peter, first Bishop of Rome, was martyred in this arena and after his death his body was claimed by Christian friends for burial in the public cemetery nearby. On the Via Cornelia, a road running directly along the stadium's northern wall, there was a cluster of tombs, most of them pagan, some of them Christian. Among these Peter was interred. And from that time on members of the small but growing Christian community in the city would daily, unless prevented by the authorities of the state, make a pilgrimage to the site of Peter's final resting place. Peter's second successor, Cletus (or Anacletus) marked the grave with a small monument. He and many others among St. Peter's early successors were interred close to the grave of the first Pontiff. (The subject of Peter's tomb is discussed at length in the next chapter.)

Not long after he rescinded the laws against Christianity and became a Christian himself, Constantine commissioned the building of a great basilica over the grave of the Apostle Peter and another above the tomb of St. Paul on the Ostian Way.

Completed in 326 and consecrated by Pope Sylvester on November 18 of that year, the first St. Peter's Basilica lasted twelve centuries before it fell into irreparable decay and was torn down to make way for the current Petrine basilica. The immense and splendid shrine to Paul survived until the early nineteenth century when it was destroyed by a fire. Its imposing replacement is true to the style and beauty of the original.

Even before commissioning the two great shrines, however, the Emperor Constantine had granted to the Church and Her Pontiff a sizeable piece of property in the southwest end of the city. This neighborhood was known as the Lateran district, for the noble family of the Laterani once owned this property until it was confiscated by Nero. Here was built the diocesan cathedral of Rome, St. John's, and adjoining it a palace for use as the Bishop's residence. San Giovanni in Laterano remains to our own time the cathedral of Rome.

For centuries after the Constantinian era the Popes continued to live in the Lateran. They would visit St. Peter's to conduct solemn pontifical ceremonies there on certain feast days but would then return to the Lateran residence.

As long as the Roman Empire existed, the Pope as Bishop of Rome was protected by the Empire's might. But in the chaotic twilight of Imperium Romanum the

Emperor ruled from far off Constantinople. This rendered the Pontiff and his city quite vulnerable to the predatory tribes that abounded in Europe during that period. Following a number of barbaric invasions which greatly imperiled the freedom of the Holy See, Pope Stephen III, in 754, made a hurried trip to France where, in robes of deep mourning and with his head covered with ashes to dramatize the plight of the Chair of Peter, he fell at the feet of the Christian king, Pepin, father of Charlemagne. The Holy Father implored the king, "in the name of God and His apostles," to intervene and save the "affairs of Sts. Peter and Paul and those of the Holy City of Rome." Whereupon Pepin led a formidable force of Franks back over the snowcapped Alps into Italy and down to Rome where they routed the hated Lombards. Following this, Pepin bestowed a large portion of land in central Italy upon the See of Peter. Covering 17,000 square miles from Umbria to Lazio, with a population of several million, the territory was to survive the next eleven centuries under the name of the Papal States. Thus, Stephen III, lover of the poor and true defender of the people became the first of the pope-kings and Pepin let it be known that France would come to the aid of its newly created ally at the first sign of hostilities against it. (Later, in the thirteenth century, the city of Avignon and the surrounding area in southern France were added to the Papal States. And it was to Avignon that Pope Clement V in 1305, in the face of political, social and economic chaos in Italy, moved the Papal throne. For the next seventy years the seat of the Papacy remained there on the banks of the Rhone, until a Dominican nun, Catherine of Siena, persuaded Pope Gregory XI to shift the headquarters of the universal church back to the left bank of the Tiber.) From early on in their existence, however, the Papal States were to come under repeated assaults from various European belligerents, causing Pope Leo IV to enclose the sacred Vatican territory with soaring brick walls, since that part of the Church's land lay at the end of the old north highway, Via Aurelia, and was most vulnerable to attack from the north. (Hence, the little enclave is known even to this day by some students of the Papacy as the Leonine City.)

Still the Lateran remained as the official Papal residence. But after Pope Gregory XI terminated the Avignon chapter of Papal history and returned to Rome he took up residence at the fortified Vatican. It is at this juncture that the history of today's Vatican City truly begins. It is from this point on, with but few exceptions, that the Vatican would be the home of the Holy Father.

Today Vatican City is an independent state *(Stato della Città del Vaticano)* and is all that is left of the sprawling Papal States that developed in the Middle Ages. When the latter were confiscated and absorbed into the new kingdom of Italy in 1870 the revolutionaries left the Pope the Vatican enclave from which to conduct the affairs of the Universal Church.

The Pontiff at the time, Pope Pius IX, refused to accept the conditions, and he and his successors to Benedict XV, severed relations with the Italian State and confined themselves to the Vatican, bitterly denouncing the "usurpers" from behind Leo IV's walls.

Under Pius XI, though, the Church ended her estrangement with Italy through the Lateran Agreement of February 11, 1929, which prescribed the present boundaries of Papal territory and resulted in the State of the City of the Vatican and the official recognition of the Pope as its Monarch, making it possible for the Papacy to function legally, rather than as a monarchy in exile, both in Italy and under international law.

In addition to the Vatican proper the Church was granted numerous extraterritorial properties in and around Rome. The most important of these are the other major basilicas besides St. Peter's, i.e., Santa Maria Maggiore on the Esquiline, San Giovanni in the Lateran, San Paolo outside the walls in Via Ostiense. Also Santa Maria in Trastevere, the Chancery of the Rome Diocese (the *Palazzo Cancelleria),* the headquarters of Propaganda Fide and other Curia buildings, and *San Lorenzo Fuori Le Mura* (Saint Lawrence's Outside the Walls) in Via Tiburtina. Enjoying the same extra-territoriality status is the Papal Villa in Castel Gandolfo, a sleepy village in the picturesque Alban Hills and summer residence of the Popes for the last several centuries. The catacombs, some colleges, and a few seminaries in the city come under the same classification.

Vatican City possesses all the characteristics of a sovereign nation. It has, for example, its own monetary system, its own postal service, its own flag and anthem. The Vatican state flag is divided vertically into two fields: yellow on the left and white on the right. In the center of the white field are the papal symbols of a tiara and two crossed keys. To honor the golden anniversary of Pius IX's ordination, Charles Gounod composed a "Papal March" which was subsequently adopted as the official state anthem. There are also the Vatican Radio, the daily newspaper, *Osservatore Romano,* the railroad, the military (the Swiss Guard), and the police *(the Vigilanza Vaticana).* Other facilities include a new garage to service cars and trucks, a few apartment houses for some of the employees, barracks for the Swiss Guard, a heliport, a fire station, several office buildings, a mosaic workshop, a marble cutter's establishment, and a seminary. There is even a parish church for the residents and workers of Vatican City, not grand St. Peter's but little St. Anne's, just inside the gate by the same name.

The Vatican is a free port and its employees buy tax-free food in the commissary and fuel at the gasoline pumps. And there is the State Department which maintains diplomatic ties with other nations.

The Pope is the sovereign of the state and all permanent citizens (about 1,500 clerics, lay staff, and domestics) owe allegiance to the Pope as a temporal ruler. Foreign heads of state make official calls on the Pope, and he, in turn, is received wherever he travels not only as a spiritual leader but also as a head of state. For example, President Carter received, with the same ceremonial trappings accorded other leaders, John Paul II at the White House in October of 1979. In the Spring of the following year the President, during a trip to Italy on N.A.T.O. matters, made an official call at the Apostolic Palace. But while the Holy Father technically possesses full legislative, executive, and judicial powers, these are, in practice, entrusted to the Pontifical Commission for the Administration of Vatican City.

And like any other sovereign nation, the little enclave called Vatican City has its border checkpoints. While the public has free access to the Square of St. Peter at all times and to the Basilica during the hours it is open, and for a small fee may visit the Vatican museums—a tour which generally includes a visit to the Sistine Chapel—between nine a.m. and one p.m. daily, one must demonstrate a legitimate purpose and present credentials in order to be admitted to the other areas of the mini-country.

There are four entrances into the non-public areas of the Vatican: The Porta Sant'Anna along Via Porta Angelica which runs behind the right colonnade (as you face the Basilica); the Porta di Bronzo, at the Basilica end of the same colonnade, to be used by those attending a private Papal audience in one of the chambers in the Apostolic Palace; the Porta della Campana (Gate of the Big Bell), so named because of its location below and just to the left of the Basilica's bell tower; and the Porta dell'Aula delle Udienze (Gate of the Audience Hall) behind the left colonnade in the Piazza del Sant'Uffizio which one uses in going to a public audience in the magnificent new ten thousand seat auditorium.

All of these Vatican borders are patrolled by the colorfully-clad Swiss Guards. In 1503 Pope Julius II, the "warrior Pope," petitioned the Swiss nation for a detachment of its best soldiers, that they might help in the defense of the perpetually threatened Papal States. Two hundred troops were soon after dispatched to the Vatican. In 1527 their military skills and loyalty to the Holy Father were put to the acid test as German and Spanish forces attacked the Vatican and Pope Clement VII. Fighting valiantly but losing about three-fourths of their meager ranks, they held the foe long enough for His Holiness and many in his court to flee along the ramparts connecting the Vatican with the fortress-like Castel Sant'Angelo (Hadrian's Tomb) on the banks of the Tiber.

Since that time the Swiss Guard, in impressive uniforms said to have been designed by Michelangelo, have had the privilege of protecting the property of the church and the person of the Pontiff.

They are aided in their cause by another security force called the Vigilanza Vaticana. While today some of the duties of the Swiss Guard are somewhat ceremonial, standing at the Vatican gates or during Pontifical rituals in their resplendent uniforms with halberds and pikes, there is nothing ceremonial about the work of the Vigilanza. These husky gents, some in navy blue suits with only a small insignia over the breast pocket turning them into uniforms, the others in plainclothes, are dedicated to their serious and sometimes dangerous task of maintaining order and protecting the Vatican and the Pope from crackpots.

(My family and I have some very close social friends on the Vigilanza. One of them in 1974, at great danger to himself, disarmed a madman who was hacking away at the Pietà with a sledgehammer and thus saved one of the greatest works of art in the history of the world. One summer day in 1975 we attended an audience at Castel Gandolfo and immediately afterwards saw another one of our friends in the Vigilanza, obviously shaken over something and holding his right hand in a handkerchief. When we inquired we learned that, all in the line of duty, he had had his eye on a potential troublemaker throughout the audience and when it seemed the latter was about to stand and yell and throw something at the Pontiff our friend moved in to muffle and disarm him and remove him, almost unnoticed, from the hall. It was then that the guard showed us the teethmarks deep in his thick fingers.)

Preeminent among the landmarks of the Vatican is, of course, the enormous Basilica of St. Peter. Facing an

immense square, St. Peter's represents Mother Church
and in the same symbolism the majestic colonnades by
Bernini are Her arms swinging open to embrace Her
sons and daughters and people of all other faiths as
well, sweeping them up into her heart, the sanctuary of
St. Peter's.

St. Peter's Basilica soars nearly five hundred feet
over the tomb of Christ's first Vicar on earth. Here
the most important Papal ceremonies—coronations,
funerals, beatifications, canonizations, consistories
—are held. It was more than a hundred years in the
building and over that span the greatest names in art
and architecture participated in its construction and
ornamentation, names like Michelangelo, Bramante,
Raphael, Sangallo and Peruzzi.

Covering an area of fifteen thousand square meters,
it is by far the largest house of worship on earth. Its interior is dominated by Bernini's ten-story high *baldacchino* (bronze canopy) over the main altar. In a side
chapel in the rear are reliquaries containing such
sacred relics as a part of the True Cross, a section of the
lance that pierced Christ's side, and Veronica's veil. At
the far wall of the apse is the bronze-encased wooden
episcopal chair actually used by the first Bishop of
Rome, held aloft by likenesses of Sts. Ambrose,
Augustine, Athanasius, and Chrysostom.

Second in prominence to the Basilica is the Apostolic
Palace. Pope Symmachus in the early sixth century built
a residence adjacent to the first St. Peter's Basilica so
that the Pontiff could have a place to stay overnight
whenever the ceremonies in St. Peter's were to take
place over a number of days. But the present complex of
buildings which make up the *Palazzo Apostolico* was
begun under Pope Sixtus V (1585-1590) and continued
under Clement VIII (1592-1605), and Paul V (1605-1621).

Containing more than eleven hundred rooms, including the Vatican Museum and Library, the Palace is
graced by the murals of the most celebrated Renaissance artists. Particularly noteworthy are the
Stanze (rooms) of Raphael. The Museum holds artistic

treasures of numerous ancient civilizations—Egypt, Eturia, Greece, and Rome among them—and the Vatican Library is the repository of thousands of the most priceless ancient manuscripts. The *Pinacoteca* (picture gallery) houses works by the masters of many nations from many ages. Then, of course, there is the Vatican's artistic *pièce de resistance,* the Sistine Chapel. Named for Pope Sixtus IV who had it built for use as the Pope's private chapel, the Sistine has been immortalized by Michelangelo's ceiling frescoes and by the terrible beauty of his Last Judgment in back of the altar.

For these reasons, the Vatican is looked upon not only as the administrative center of the Universal Church but also as one of the outstanding centers of culture and learning in the world.

The Apostolic Palace also encompasses a number of lovely—and large—courtyards such as the *Cortile di San Damaso* and those of the *Belvedere* and the *Pigna.* The private apartment of the Pope is on the top floor of the section overlooking St. Peter's Square from behind the colonnade.

The Vatican Gardens are among the loveliest to be found in all of Europe. With their lush vegetation, shaded promenades, graceful arboreta, murmuring fountains, marble statuary, and indescribably beautiful views of the dome, these gardens have been like the "still waters" of the Twenty-third Psalm, restoring the soul and body of each Holy Father for half a millennium now. Two favorite stops of ours in the gardens are the *Casina* or little stone summer house built in their midst by Pius IV, and the perfect replica of the grotto at Lourdes. The Casina now houses the Pontifical Academy of Sciences.

On the far edge of the gardens is the Vatican radio station with its lofty transmitting tower in the form of a steel cross. A number of times my family and I have been strolling in the gardens with some Vatican friends when the station was just beginning its day's broadcasting activities and we could hear the theme song: *Christus Vincit! Christus Regnat! Christus Imperat!*

(Another pleasant sight is that of the seminarians at the Ethiopian College, located also on the edge of the Vatican Gardens, clothed in cassocks no matter what the weather and laughingly kicking a soccer ball around for diversion between classes.)

Midst all this splendor resides the Pope but in monastic frugality and simplicity. The humble Papal apartment of bedroom, study, and chapel is on the top floor of the Apostolic Palace overlooking St. Peter's Square from behind the colonnade.

It will be our aim in a later chapter to provide a look at the Pope's day-to-day activity and at least a glimpse at his precious few private moments.

2

In Search of the First Pontiff

How appropriate it is that the Supreme Pontiff of Mother Church reside and carry out his work in the Vatican. For in this hallowed soil repose the remains of St. Peter, the man who walked with Jesus, the apostle to whom Our Lord entrusted the keys to the Kingdom, the first bishop of Rome, the first Pope. That this place was and remains the burial place of Peter can be and has been well-documented beyond all doubt.

After the great fire of Rome in July, A.D. 64, the suspected and likely arsonist, the Emperor Nero himself, put the Imperial propaganda machinery into high gear to get the word out among the surviving populace, that the conflagration had been the work of the tiny Christian community in the city. To strengthen his story he cited the "weird" rituals of the fanatical cultists, their sacrilege (by worshiping not the pagan deities of the Roman pantheon but a "ridiculous" man-God instead), their disloyalty to the State. As a clincher, Nero charged the followers of Christ with many other heinous crimes including cannibalism. To support the last allegation he quoted from Christian writings: "Unless you eat My flesh and drink My blood you shall not have life in you."

The deranged tyrant had the Senate enact legislation outlawing Christianity as a subversive organization. He issued a warrant for the arrest of the leaders of the "organization" and launched the first persecution of the Christians. Eventually the first Supreme Pontiff, Peter the Apostle, was brought, in chains, to the unspeakable horror of the Mamertine Prison adjacent to the Forum. The other prominent Christian leader at that time, Paul, was also soon incarcerated in the same foul dungeon.

For nine months Peter and Paul suffered the brutalities of the jail guards and then were informed that Nero had given the word for their execution. Paul, who by virtue of his provincial Roman citizenship was entitled to a dignified execution, was taken outside the city walls about a mile down the Ostian Road and decapitated. Peter, along with some of his flock, was crucified before an enormous crowd jammed into the stadium known as the Circus of Nero on the southern slope of Vatican Hill. Behind the stadium was a public cemetery of streets lined with the mausolea of pagan Romans. Adjoining these streets was a sort of potter's field where the grieving friends of the Apostle interred his remains.

For the next quarter of a century or so, the location of the grave was marked, as a safeguard against desecration, only in the memories of these Christians. During this period too, an unofficial Christian cemetery developed around the grave of Peter since many had before their martyrdom made it known that they wished to lie forever near their beloved bishop.

When in A.D. 90 the first pogrom against the Christians had abated somewhat, Anacletus, the Bishop of Rome and second successor to St. Peter, built a small, unostentatious shrine directly over the grave of Peter. To this point would come, daily, groups of Christians in pious pilgrimage (a practice which continues down to our very own day). One of the marks of a true Christian from early on has been the desire to walk with Jesus. Consequently, across the last two millennia untold millions have come to Rome from around the globe to cross the Tiber and approach the tomb of the one who walked nearest to Our Lord on earth, feeling that this is as close as they might get bodily to Jesus until the second coming. These transpontine pilgrimages would in the early centuries, cease each time a new wave of anti-Christian atrocities would be started by the state. Yet as much as the government wished to suppress the infant religion it would not go so far as to desecrate or destroy the grave of Peter in compliance with its own statute, *Violatio Sepulchri,* which declared all burial grounds—Pagan, Jewish, Christian alike—to be inviolable.

A persistent tradition tells us however that the persecution of Valerian in 257-258 was so savage that the Christians feared for the security of the Apostle's mortal remains and secretly exhumed them for transferal to the Catacombs of St. Sebastian on the Appian Way. Graffiti and inscriptions in these catacombs (one reads: *Domus Petri,* Home of Peter) seem to corroborate the claim by some scholars that Peter was for a short period entombed therein. Valerian did confiscate all Christian cemeteries during his persecution but when, under his successor Gallienus, these grounds were restored to the Christian community, the apostle's relics were re-interred in their original grave which was still indicated by a memorial.

A letter from about the year 200 by a certain *Roman presbyter* (priest) named Gaius perhaps refers to this shrine. From the letter and later archeological evidence we learn that the Christian community in time built a brick wall around their potter's field to prevent further encroachment on it by pagan mausolea. Since the wall actually crossed directly over the Apostle's tomb, it incorporated into its fabric at that point a "trophy" as Gaius calls it. (*Trophy,* in the ancient idiom, meant monument.) This was either the memorial erected by Pope Anacletus or a later one. From a manufacturer's stamp in the tile of a drain in this plot it can be plausibly inferred that the wall project dates to about A.D. 150.

(The final resting place of the Fisherman of Galilee would continue to be marked and exalted monumentally through the ages, in the fourth century by a monument of fine gray marble built by Constantine as the focal point of his basilica in honor of Peter, in the Middle Ages by numerous altars superimposed one upon the other, in the sixteenth century by the soaring cupola of Michelangelo, and lastly, in 1633 by the imposing bronze canopy of Bernini.)

With the victory of Constantine over Maxentius in the famous battle of the Milvian Bridge there opened a new chapter in the history of Rome and of Christianity. Crediting the Christians' God for his victory, Constantine in gratitude gave properties (the Lateran and the Vatican) to the beleaguered community, ordered a temple built over the site of Christ's tomb on Golgotha, and in 326 began the building of an immense, five-aisle basilica to honor the founder of the Church, with its main altar to be placed directly over the little oratory of Anacletus. (At this time he also commissioned a basilica to be erected over the tomb of Paul on Via Ostiense.) His Imperial Majesty participated in the work with his own hands, at one point symbolically removing twelve baskets of earth in honor of the twelve Apostles. A huge portion of Vatican Hill had to be cut away so that the church might be situated over the grave site.

Tradition informs us that Constantine was most reverential in caring for the holy remains. The *Liber Pontificalis* describes how the tomb of the Apostle was opened in the presence of Pope St. Sylvester and the Emperor, the bones collected and placed in a small but precious chest of gilt bronze surmounted by a solid gold cross weighing 160 pounds, and entombed beneath the main altar of the massive church. Throughout the rest of his life Constantine continued to ornament the tomb of Peter with precious objects.

In 594, due to the troubled times, Pope Gregory the Great ordered the raising of the basilica's floor so that the Apostolic tomb, now a veritable repository of gold and silver and jewels, might be more secure out of sight. It could now be viewed only by going through a passage in the crypt beneath the church. (Subsequent floor elevations and new altars by later Popes, Clement VIII for one, put the tomb of Peter even further underground.)

Throughout the barbaric invasions that brought the once proud capital to its knees in the fifth and sixth centuries, the tomb of Peter was spared desecration principally because the invaders were themselves Christian. But in 846 the hapless Eternal City was plundered by the non-Christian Saracens who wrecked everything in their violent path and even plundered the temple and profaned the tomb of Peter. From this point on there was to be no trace of Constantine's gold cross and precious stones.

After the departure of the merciless Saracens the damages to the great basilica were repaired by Pope Leo IV. Nearly all of Leo's successors continued to embellish the ancient church with rare and costly productions of old and contemporary Christian art. And all the European nations which had by now been illuminated by the glow of Christianity also sent marvelous gifts of art to enrich St. Peter's.

The 1300's marked the beginning of another significant chapter in the basilica's history. Upon the election of the French Pope, Clement V, as mentioned in the previous chapter, the Papal residence was transferred —for political reasons too involved for this volume to treat—from Rome to the sleepy town of Avignon in southern France. (The seventy years that the Papacy remained there have often been referred to by Catholic writers as the "Babylonian Captivity.") During that sad time St. Peter's fell dark and abandoned. From sheer neglect the basilica began to deteriorate. Its south wall bulged outward more than six feet out of true and the roof started to collapse. When Pope Gregory XI brought the Papal throne back to Rome in 1378, it was too late to save the crumbling basilica.

Finally in 1450, the decay of St. Peter's had reached such alarming dimensions that the architects of Pope Nicholas V exhorted him to raze the sacred edifice lest it someday fall down upon the Holy Father and his flock.

But Nicholas died before he could carry out his intention to level the old structure and replace it with a far more splendorous one. It wasn't until eight Popes and more than a half century later that the Constantinian basilica was pulled down to make way for the magnificent St. Peter's we know and love today.

The passage of so many centuries notwithstanding, Catholic tradition continued to hold that St. Peter's Church—both the old and the new—stood expressly as a monument over the grave of the Apostolic Prince. In 1939 the newly elected Pope Pius XII had the faith and the fortitude to put this tradition to the test. As preparations were being made in the grottoes under the basilica for the tomb of his predecessor, Pius XI, the digging had accidentally led to the discovery of an ancient pagan burial ground. Pius XII, *Papa Pacelli* as the Romans affectionately called their own native son, then authorized further excavations far below the nave of the church and gave orders for a specific search for the tomb of St. Peter.

(Previous Pontiffs had shied away from such a quest. One deterrent was the frightening warning by Gregory the Great way back in 594 that anyone who would commit such a sacrilege as to disturb the bones of the Apostle would suffer aweful consequences. Another was the well-documented calamity, coincidental or not, that accompanied the last disturbance of the holy earth around Peter's grave. When Bernini informed Clement VIII that the heavy columns supporting his proposed bronze baldacchino would need strong and deep foundations that required extensive digging near the Apostolic tomb, the Holy Father, acutely aware of Gregory's curse, was most reluctant to grant permission. Bernini prevailed. Work was initiated, auspiciously, on the Feast of Peter and Paul. Within a week the foreman in charge of the work dropped dead. Hours later his assistant passed away. Hysteria swept over Rome and intensified when a few days later another official involved in the operation died. When the Pontiff himself took seriously ill a short time later, all the laborers walked off the job, terrified by the omens. Eventually the panic eased, Rome regained its composure, and Bernini via a promise of pay raises was able to get the diggers back to the task.)

Pius XII's excavators found a cemeterial street lined with house-like sepulchers whose interiors contained niches with urns of ashes or bones of Romans from the Imperial Age. At the very least, this supported the long-standing belief that Constantine had built the original St. Peter's over a cemetery.

The excitement in the Vatican became almost unbearable when early in the digging, deep and directly under the Papal altar a small, ruined, immured monument was uncovered, fitting the description of Gaius' "trophy." More exciting still, however, was the slab, undoubtedly a gravestone, found at the foot of this wall shrine. When upon raising the stone the excavators unfortunately found an empty grave, the long trail seemed to have come to a hopeless dead end. Any further probing appeared senseless.

But a humble, learned professor from the University of Rome, Margherita Guarducci, was granted permission by Pius XII to continue the search. An expert in ancient graffiti, she spent the next six years scrutinizing the crude etchings on the wall above and near the vacant grave. Professor Guarducci in her customary scholarly thoroughness wandered throughout the catacombs of Rome comparing the etchings with the graffiti of the subterranean galleries to further authenticate the former. She sought the opinions of colleagues, cross-examined archeologists who had worked on the initial project, consulted endless volumes of early Christian writings. The tenacious and tireless woman grew more convinced with time that she was on the right trail. One day she deciphered a Greek inscription near a recess in a side wall. It gave this chilling and thrilling simple message: "Peter is within." Now Professor Guarducci examined the recess itself and was persuaded that it was indeed an ossuary, i.e., a burial niche for human bones. And though Constantine's marble enclosure of this original shrine was gone, it would have doubtlessly incorporated this side wall too.

So then, the niche was empty? Another dead end? Not to the dedicated detective. Interrogating workmen who had helped in the digging from the start, she learned that a monsignor assigned to the excavation work had, some ten years earlier, come upon some bones in the niche in question, gathered them in a box, and moved them to a nearby storage room. By this time Pius XII and his successor John XXIII had entered the ages and it was Pope Paul VI who authorized the professor to try to identify the relics. With the aid of fellow scholars from the university, Guarducci determined the bones to be those of a man of sixty or seventy. In the chest with the bones there had been found also some handfuls of dirt and shreds of purple and gold cloth. All of this, plus the inscriptions, plus what ancient writings and tradition had to say on the matter added up to one irrefutable fact as far as Professor Guarducci was concerned: Here indeed were the mortal remains of Peter the Apostle!

Tradition teaches that he would have been about seventy years of age at his death and that he was buried in the earth. Constantine in encasing the remains would appropriately have wrapped them in precious cloth. As for the remains being found in a place other than that marked by Anacletus was simple to explain. In an age where grave robbing and desecration was virtually a national pastime, Constantine, or someone in charge of the basilica soon after him, would likely have taken the precaution of transferring the holy relics to a safe, clandestine place nearby.

The evidence was persuasive enough to Pope Paul VI. On the morning of June 26, 1968, at a splendid ceremony in the basilica, he settled the issue for the Catholic world. From the Papal Altar, sunlit by golden beams streaming through the little windows of Michelangelo's dome, beneath the towering letters at the base of the cupola declaring: "TU ES PETRUS....", the Holy Father,

262nd successor to the Apostle announced that the remains of St. Peter had been found.

Now the bones repose once again in their original secret niche. Except for scholars cleared for serious research by the Vatican Commission of Sacred Archeology there is usually no access to the excavations beneath St. Peter's. I was fortunate during my Fulbright studies in Rome to have had the unforgettable spiritual experience of approaching the tomb of Peter. Most other visitors to this holy place must content themselves with a stop in the little chapel in honor of Peter down in the basilica's grottoes, the altar of which is situated but a few feet above the niche.

So then, on your first (or next) visit to St. Peter's Basilica look for a stairwell marked *Tombe dei Papi,* just to the left front of the main altar and descend it. Follow the narrow corridor, perhaps thirty yards, to the iron-gated chapel to Peter on the right. (Directly across the hallway you will see a brightly lit alcove with the sarcophagus of Pope Pius XII whose faith and courage paved the way for the inspiring discovery.) Enter the chapel and pray at the little altar and you will be but a few feet from the body of St. Peter.

You will be perpetuating a pilgrimage that began nearly two thousand years ago. You will be in the company of one who so often enjoyed the company of Our Lord. You will be at the heart and center of all Christendom. You will, more than ever before, realize the true, full, and eternal significance of the words: "THOU ART PETER AND UPON THIS ROCK I SHALL BUILD MY CHURCH."

3

The Sacred College

The Supreme Pontiff has primacy of jurisdiction over the Universal Church. Assisting and advising him in the full range of ecclesiastical affairs are the cardinals, prelates who either head the various secretariates, congregations, and tribunals of the Roman Curia (the Pope's cabinet), or administer important sees (dioceses or archdioceses) around the world. They make up the Sacred College of Cardinals which some like to call the Church's Senate.

Though the cardinalate did not evolve into its present form until the late twelfth century, it has its roots in old Rome. Though the bloody persecutions ceased in the early three hundreds, the next several centuries remained quite perilous for the Church. Therefore, the Popes in those times relied heavily on the wise counsel of influential men who helped to swing the Church toward safety and away from trouble. In the sixth century these priests and laymen who so helped the Pontiff came to be known as cardinals (from the Latin *cardo* meaning hinge).

Since it was common practice for the Bishop of Rome to consult with the city's clergy in all crucial diocesan matters, ultimately all the pastors of the many Roman parishes were given the title of cardinal. In addition to these, the Holy Father also sought the opinions of the lay deacons who directed the numerous Church dispensaries for the poor, ill, hungry, displaced persons in and around the old city. And so they too were called cardinals.

Then when there was the occasion to issue an edict or rule on some problem affecting the world-wide Church, the Bishop of Rome would often consult with neighboring prelates, usually the bishops of the suburbicarian episcopates of Ostia, Palestrina, Porto, Albano, Velletri, Frascati, and Sabina. They too then, logically, were referred to as cardinals, or those upon whom the welfare of the Church "hinged."

Thus though the order of cardinals was a loosely organized one in its early history and had no clearly defined roles other than to give counsel to the Pope when he sought it, from the start there were within the institution three clear and distinct divisions: cardinal-bishops, cardinal-priests, and cardinal-deacons. And though the Sacred College has been constituted as we now know it for eight centuries, it still consists of those same three branches.

As the centuries rolled by, the Church, as prophesied, spread to all lands. Since the Popes could not possibly travel to all of these far-flung places they needed delegates who would be authorized to speak for them to help maintain a dialogue between Rome and the Churches of the various nations. Usually they would draw from the ranks of the cardinals for these delegates. This practice was the forerunner of the agency of the Papal Secretariat of State, which in function became like the state department or foreign ministry of any nation.

With the continued expansion of the Church geographically, there was a concomitant expansion of the Church bureaucracy and with this the Chair of Peter looked more and more for help from the cardinals.

In 1059 Pope Nicholas II expanded the realm of the cardinalate, heretofore an exclusively Roman domain, sixty miles beyond the area of the Eternal City by making Desiderius, the holy abbot of the Benedictine Monastery at Monte Cassino, a cardinal. But to maintain the ancient and traditional character of the institution, the Holy Father gave Desiderius the pastorate of one of Rome's parishes, thus making him, if only in a symbolic way, a cardinal-priest of Rome.

That same year saw the cardinals become more important to the Church than ever before when Pope Nicholas put into their hands the privilege of electing the Pope.

Toward the end of the twelfth century, Pope Alexander III appointed the first cardinal outside of Italy, making a German archbishop a titular pastor of a Roman Church.

While the Code of Canon Law promulgated in 1918 decreed that all cardinals must from then on be ordained priests (Pius IX's secretary of state, Cardinal Giacomo Antonelli was a layman) and though Pope John decreed that henceforth every cardinal, if not already a bishop, must be consecrated as such immediately after his elevation to the College, there remain the sometimes confusing distinctions of cardinal-bishop, cardinal-priest, cardinal-deacon.

The explanation is that today's cardinal-bishops are, like their ancient forebears, the bishops of the suburbicarian sees mentioned earlier. The cardinal-priests are bishops of dioceses around the globe with titular parishes in Rome. For example the Archbishop of Boston is technically the pastor of Santa Susanna parish in the heart of Rome, the Archbishop of Los Angeles is pastor of Sant'Anastasia. But while a cardinal-priest has title to a Church in Rome he appoints a vicar to serve as *de facto* pastor. The cardinal may not get to see his parish in *Urbs Aeterna* for years at a stretch. This practice has another benefit to it for Rome besides maintaining the long traditions of the cardinalate. For many of the city's ancient and beautiful churches are often in desperate need of restoration and repair, and the cardinals, especially those from American dioceses, often turn to their affluent flocks back home to help fund such work. The late Cardinal Spellman, for example, led a fund-raising drive in his

New York Archdiocese to finance the major repairs on his lovely titular Church of Sts. John and Paul on the Coelian Hill.

Cardinal-deacon is the designation for members of the Sacred College residing in Rome and heading one of the commissions of the Church government. They constitute an analogy to the early cardinal-deacons who also directed Church agencies.

So, technically, even today when the cardinals gather in a consistory to advise a Pope, or in a conclave to elect one, they are not high-ranking prelates from around the globe but rather the pastors of Rome, along with the directors of Church agencies, along with a few neighboring bishops come together to "swing" the Church successfully through another crucial period.

In 1586 Pope Sixtus V fixed the number of cardinals at seventy, basing the figure on the appointment by Moses of seventy elders to help with the problems of the numerous Hebrew tribes. This figure remained in effect until Pope John XXIII, in the third year of his pontificate, increased the number to eighty-seven. Paul VI, following the lead of his predecessor in a move to make the college truly representative of the universal Church, raised the membership to one hundred and thirty-four.

Because the Sacred College had recently been rocked with some great scandals, i.e., at the end of the fifteenth and beginning of the sixteenth centuries, Sixtus set down a set of high moral standards for members of the Sacred College, standards that still obtain.

And to further formalize and institutionalize the cardinalate, Sixtus established fifteen congregations (committees), each with its special responsibilities, and cardinals to head and staff them. Cardinals so assigned had to reside in Rome. This was the beginning of the Roman Curia as we recognize it today. The remaining cardinals administered dioceses but had to be ready to come to Rome when needed.

In our time cardinals are still selected by the Pope for the same reasons they have always been chosen.

They are priests of outstanding learning, piety, administrative ability, organizational skills, or grasp of Canon Law. They are secondary only to His Holiness and precede all other ecclesiastical dignitaries. They are also referred to as the Princes of the Church and are accorded all the same courtesies extended to royal sons in all the diplomatic courts of the world.

Let us now consider the three-step process for the creation of cardinals.

When the Holy Father intends to name new members to the Sacred College, he holds a secret consistory, i.e., a meeting with only the cardinals in attendance. This meeting the Pope summons so that he might consult on this important step with his loyal advisors and assistants. At this assembly the Pope delivers an address, in Latin (still the official language of Mother Church and Her government), citing the names of those he intends to elevate to the cardinalate. Following this speech, he poses this question to the Papal princes: *"Quid vobis videtur?"* (How does it seem to you?)

Whereupon, unless there are some dissenters, all the cardinals rise, uncover and bow their heads in agreement.

Then the Pope makes the appointments official, proclaiming: "By the authority of Almighty God, and of the Holy Apostles Peter and Paul, and of our own, We appoint...(here he reads the list of names)...as cardinals, in the name of the Father, and of the Son, and of the Holy Spirit. Amen."

Those appointed are immediately notified of their selection by a *biglietto* or message delivered personally by an official from the Vatican Secretariat of State. Within a few days the nominees, in a simple ceremony at the Papal residence, will be given the red biretta by the Pope himself.

(In 1246 Pope Innocent IV had decided to give the cardinalate a distinctive mark in attire. He declared that all cardinals should wear a red clerical hat, pointing out that its color should serve as a constant reminder to the wearer that he should be prepared to spill his blood if need be in the defense of the Church and Her Pontiff.

Pope Boniface VIII in 1295 further ennobled the office by awarding the cardinals the red cassock. In 1495 Pope Paul II added to the cardinal's garb the red biretta and a white mitre of silk damask. Thus even today on important occasions the members of the college contribute enormously, by the splendor of their vestments, to the colorful panoply of Church ritual.)

Some time later a public consistory is held. Saint Peter's is jammed to overflowing as His Holiness in a ceremony of unforgettable solemnity confers on the new princes the broad-brimmed red *gallero,* symbol of the cardinalate. While never worn, this hat is sometimes carried behind the cardinal in solemn processions. As the ceremony closes, the Supreme Pontiff embraces each new cardinal in the kiss of peace while the entire congregation chants the beautiful hymn, *Te Deum.*

Immediately after the public consistory, the cardinals reconvene with the Pope again in a private consistory for the brief and simple ceremony of *occlusio et aperitio oris* (the closing and opening of the mouth). Here the Pope symbolically closes the mouth of each incoming member of the Sacred College while offering a prayer and then with another prayer opens the mouth of each. This is in the way of a reminder that a cardinal is expected to keep certain secrets of his high office and, when necessary, to give counsel to the Pope.

A Pope may sometimes deem it, for various reasons, injudicious to announce the name of one he has chosen for the cardinalate. He will then name that prelate only *in pectore* (in the chest or heart) hoping to divulge the name when circumstances allow. A cardinal *in pectore* has no title, rights, or functions until his name has been disclosed. But once disclosed, that cardinal enjoys precedence and seniority from the time of his secret selection. If a Pope dies without disclosing the name or names he had held *in pectore* the appointments lapse, and it is possible that these men will never gain the red hat. When Pope John XXIII died in 1963 he took the names of three cardinals *in pectore* to the tomb with him.

As we have pointed out, the members of the Sacred College are either in apostolate or in curial work. Those in the first group are dispersed throughout the world as heads of dioceses in the manner of the Apostles themselves.

Curial cardinals reside in Rome, directly assisting the Pope in the central government of the Church. It is about them and the Curia that we will speak in the following brief chapter.

4

The Curia

In his role as shepherd of the Universal Church, the Holy Father understandably must count heavily on a veritable army of assistants. Since the reign of Peter, the Supreme Pontiffs have sought in their Apostolic work the help and counsel of experts in the many fields of human endeavor into which the Church must venture.

The Vatican bureaucracy known as the Roman Curia, or simply the Curia, is the rough equivalent of the numerous departments of the executive branch of our federal government, and the heads of the various Curia congregations and secretariats the ecclesiastical counterparts of the members of the President's cabinet.

Revised most recently under Paul VI's Apostolic Constitution, *Regimini Ecclesiae Universae,* the Curia, over many centuries, evolved from the assemblies of the Roman clergy that the early Popes looked to for assistance in their administrative duties. But it was the sixteenth century that saw the Curia take shape as we understand it in our day. And from the efficient organizational reforms in Church government of Sixtus V evolved the congregations of the Roman Curia, though the actual roots of some of the departments can be traced as far back as the early thirteenth century.

In its new post-Vatican II form, the Roman Curia is far more international in character than it had ever been. Heretofore the real control of it resided in the hands of the Italians in the Sacred College.

The Curia consists first and foremost of the Holy Office of the Pope, part of which is the Secretariat of State and another part of which is the Council for the Public Affairs of the Church. Because of their importance the office complexes of both State and Public Affairs are located near the Pope's private quarters. They are to be found on the third loggia of the Apostolic Palace, overlooking the San Damaso courtyard.

The Secretariat of State is the chief agency for carrying out the Pope's policies and for fostering good relations between the Vatican and other nations. At its head is the Cardinal Secretary of State who ranks, if not by Church law, at least certainly in practice, second only to the Pope in the hierarchy. At meetings of all the heads of the different ministries within the Curia he presides. Even the Secretariat of State's companion department within the Papal office, the Council for Public Affairs, is under his ultimate jurisdiction. The Secretary of State is aided by a *Sostituto* or Substitute of the Secretariat of State in his endless and monumental duties.

The Secretariat maintains an articulation with the other branches of the Curia, with the bishops around the world, with representatives of the Holy See stationed in foreign lands and with governments who have diplomatic ties with the Holy See. It is also responsible for the training and assigning of diplomats in the Vatican service.

A number of our recent pontiffs, most notably Pius XII and John XXIII, arrived at the Chair of Peter through long and distinguished diplomatic careers. The representative of the Pope in a foreign country may be a Legate (usually a cardinal), the highest rank, or a Nuncio, an official with diplomatic standing, who deals both with the Catholic bishops and the civil government of the country to which the Pope has sent him. Sometimes the Pope wishes to have his representative deal only with the Catholic bishops of a country and not with the civil government. In that case he will send a representative with the rank of Apostolic Delegate.

While a papal diplomatic service might seem more temporal than spiritual the reality is that the Vatican has no foreign policy as such but still perpetuates diplomatic relations with other lands in order to promote better conditions for the saving of souls around the globe. Thus, the modern Vatican regards the diplomats accredited to it as being there not because the Pope is head of a miniature state but out of deference to his spiritual position.

Two Vatican publications come out of the State Secretariat: the *Acta Apostolicae Sedes* (a chronicle of Church government activities) and the *Annuario Pontificio* (Papal yearbook). Problems of particular sensitivity for the Holy See—peace, disarmament, human rights, the poor, the starving—come under the purview of this department.

The Curia also consists of the Sacred Congregations which are, in fact, the Pope's ministries. In our time they are ten in number, each with a distinct field of competence, and each with a cardinal prefect at its head. Let us look briefly at each.

The Sacred Congregation for the Doctrine of the Faith established in 1542 as the *Holy Office,* has even deeper roots in the *Holy Office of the Inquisition* set up by Pope Innocent III in the beginning of the thirteenth century to fight heresy. While its *raison d'etre* continues to be the defense of the Faith, the congregation was given a new name and a more positive orientation of promoting orthodox doctrine—and in so doing fighting heresy—by Pope Paul VI. The dominion of this congregation encompasses all questions of faith and morals. Its offices are housed in the huge yellowish travertine edifice in *Piazza del Sant'Uffizio* just beyond the west arm of the colonnade of St. Peter's Square. (Almost all the other congregations of the Curia have their headquarters in the twin buildings of Piazza Pio XII between St. Peter's

Square and the Via della Conciliazione which slopes lazily down to the lazy old Tiber.)

The Sacred Congregation for Bishops, previously named the Consistorial Congregation, was established in 1588. Its scope of competence covers the establishment and territorial redistribution of dioceses, the nomination of bishops and lesser prelates, the supervision of the pastoral work of bishops, the care of them in retirement, the supervision of bishops' councils, the publication and dissemination of pastoral norms and guidelines for bishops.

The Sacred Congregation for the Eastern Churches dates from 1862, under Pius IX, and has competence in matters concerning the Catholic laity and clergy of the Eastern Rite Churches spread around the world.

The Sacred Congregation for the Sacraments and Divine Worship deals with all questions concerning the seven sacraments and divine worship.

The Sacred Congregation for the Clergy serves the clergy, fosters programs to help the priests in their spirituality, preaching and catechetical activities. Originally known as the Congregation of the Council, it was set up in 1564 for the express purpose of implementing the norms drafted at the Council of Trent. (For more than a decade the prefect of this congregation was the American John Cardinal Wright of Pittsburgh, who passed away in 1979.)

The Sacred Congregation for Religious and Secular Institutes concerns itself with the activities and disciplined behavior of the religious orders of men and women as well as with those of secular institutes especially with respect to adherence to orthodox doctrine.

The Sacred Congregation for the Evangelization of Peoples (which still retains as an alternate name *Propaganda Fide)* is situated across from the Spanish Steps in Piazza di Spagna. It is charged, as its old Latin name suggests, with spreading the gospel to all lands. It supervises the mission programs of the Church.

The Sacred Congregation for the Causes of the Saints studies the causes of prospective saints, conducts investigations to determine the sanctity of their lives and the validity of miracles attributed to their intercession. In addition, this congregation oversees the procedures for both beatification and canonization.

The Sacred Congregation for Catholic Education has supervisory competence over Catholic seminaries, universities, schools and all other institutes of Catholic learning.

Along with these ten congregations there are within the Curia three tribunals:

The Sacred Apostolic Penitentiary which has competence over all confessional matters.

The Supreme Tribunal of the Apostolic Signatura which is responsible for the resolution of ecclesiastical judicial controversies.

The Sacred Roman Rota which is in effect a court of appeals and largely interested in cases of marriage annulments.

There are also these three secretariats:

The Secretariat for Promoting Christian Unity, whose name clearly reveals its purpose.

The Secretariat for Non-Christians, which aims to foster an ongoing dialogue with other religions.

The Secretariat for Non-Believers, which hopes to do likewise with the adherents of atheism.

There are also in addition to the aforementioned major departments a number of offices and permanent commissions dealing with a wide range of subjects from the spiritual, moral and social problems of the family within a spiritual context to the updating of the code of Canon Law, to the administration of the Holy Father's Relief Service for the world's needy.

Recruitment to the Curia? While there is no clear-cut systematic plan for filling the curial ranks, the classic beginning for a young cleric is study at the prestigious Roman Seminary where, if he demonstrates an uncommon capacity for scholarship and long, hard work, he may attract the attention and endorsement of an influential prelate. For instance, the youthful Giovanni Montini had his entry into the Curia arranged by a Monsignor Pizzardo. Decades later the world would come to know and to remember Montini as the beloved Pope Paul VI.

What about the workday of the Vatican bureaucrats? The Curia workers, the vast majority of them clerics, toil officially until one-thirty. On your next visit to *Bella Roma* try to be in or around the Vatican at that hour on some weekday and you will see the picturesque, cobblestoned streets suddenly fill up with cassocks as cardinals, bishops, monsignori, and priests head home or to some inexpensive *trattoria*—homework in their attache cases—for a steaming hot plate of pasta, a glass of chilled Frascati, a generous cup of cappucino. After this, and perhaps a snooze and then a walk in the historic streets, they will be back in Christ's vineyards either via endless paperwork at home or committee meetings somewhere in Urbs Aeterna.

5

The Election of a Pope

From the very moment that a Pope breathes his last, the centuries-old Church machinery of the *interregnum* begins to chug gracefully again. And from this moment on, to the coronation of a successor, the functions of the cardinals and officials of the Vatican are regulated by custom and by edicts from the earliest ages of the Church.

This *interregnum* or period between the passing of one Pontiff and the election of a new one is known by the Latin term, *Sede Vacante* (Vacancy of the Holy See).

Commemorative coins are minted and stamps issued all carrying the message: Sede Vacante. *Osservatore Romano,* the Vatican daily, also announces that "The Chair is Vacant" on its masthead while its pages are bordered in black. Across the Tiber and across the world Catholics mourn and pray for the repose of the Pontiff's soul and for God's guidance and blessing upon the Church. Converging on Rome is a multitude of journalists, commentators, technicians to cover the three historic events of the funeral of the late Pope and the election and coronation of his heir. Around the clock the Vatican Radio plays solemn and mournful music interrupted only by special bulletins. Papal power has returned to Christ in Heaven and so the Sacred Congregations of the Church government limit their activity to the most routine matters. No bulls, briefs, concordats, nothing of consequence may be signed. For while the cardinals are the trustees of Papal power they cannot exercise it.

Centuries old rituals are renewed the instant the Holy Father passes away.

Immediately after the Papal physicians have determined that the Pope has expired it falls to the Cardinal *Camerlengo* to conduct a solemn ritual through which he will announce the sad news. (The Camerlengo is the member of the Sacred College who administers the property and finances of the Holy See. At the death of the Pope, he becomes head of the College of Cardinals and among his many duties is the task of summoning all the members to a conclave for the election of a successor to the Chair of Peter.) Until this century the ritual called for the Camerlengo to bend over the Pope's body, lift the veil from his face, and offer prayers for the swift flight of the soul to Paradise. With all others in the room kneeling, the Camerlengo was then to take a small silver hammer and tap lightly the Pope's forehead three times calling out each time in increasing decibel his surname and family name. This was followed by the sad and solemn declaration: "The Pope is truly dead." With the exception of the hammer the little ceremony has remained intact up to our own day.

Now the fisherman's ring is slipped from the Pope's finger. Its seal, with the name of the Pope and likenesses of Peter and the fisherman's net, had been used countless times to authenticate Papal documents. This and other seals were used to validate Papal Bulls and various proclamations by first pressing them into red ink. Now they are all gathered and destroyed, or at least rendered unserviceable, so there can be no illegitimate use of them in the future.

Since the Camerlengo is the head of the Church *pro tempore,* though without Papal authority, he is escorted, for security's sake, everywhere he goes by two Swiss Guard officers and by plainclothes members of the Vatican *Vigilanza.*

To the bedside of the deceased Pope are now summoned the penitentiaries—the black-robed Franciscans who hear confessions in many languages in the Basilica. Their task is to wash the Pontiff's mortal remains and, following the embalming, vest the Holy Father to lie in state.

Meanwhile the Camerlengo notifies the Cardinal Vicar to have all the church bells of Rome toll to announce the death of His Holiness.

When the preparations are completed (on the same day if death takes place in the early morning hours), the Pope's body is removed to the Sistine Chapel where it is placed on a seven foot high, sloping, red-velveted catafalque. The Pontiff is garbed in a white soutane and on his head is the *camauro,* a crimson velvet cap.

The bier is attended by Swiss Guards and other officers of the Noble Guard and the various Vatican units. Eight tall candles, four on either side of the catafalque glimmer and cast dancing shadows upon the altar's wondrous backdrop, the magnificent Last Judgment of Michelangelo. In this most fitting scene the Pope passes his first night in eternity and continues to lie in state the following day. That evening the body is borne in a solemn funeral procession, to the accompaniment of the tolling bells, through silent multitudes in the vast square. Now vested in resplendent Pontifical robes the chief priest makes his last solemn entry into his cathedral where he will lie in state another three days. The body, upon the catafalque, is positioned at the end of the center aisle for visitation by the Pope's flock. And flock they do, by the tens of thousands, to bid farewell to their beloved *Santo Padre.*

Upon the death of a Pope all the members of the diplomatic corps accredited to the Holy See come to the Vatican en masse to pay tribute to the departed Bishop of Rome and to his sacred and historic office. At the bier, receiving the condolences from the dean and spokesman of the corps are two cardinals, the Camerlengo and the Secretary of State. In the early evening of the third day there takes place the solemn funeral rites. (Up to and including the rites for John XXIII, these were conducted in the Basilica, attended by just a few thousand specially invited guests. But in the case of Paul VI and also of John Paul I, in the summer of 1979, the cardinals decided on a simple requiem Mass to be held in the vast square of St. Peter's so that all who wished to could participate. A particularly poignant vignette indelibly impressed on my memory is the multitude spontaneously waving their handkerchiefs in a touching gesture of filial farewell to Paul VI as, at the end of the Mass, he was borne into the great church for the last time. Having met with such overwhelming approval and response by the faithful, this new outdoor arrangement would appear to be a permanent one, barring unfavorable weather.) *Tu es Petrus* chants the Sistine Choir while the bells throughout all of Rome toll. A cardinal then steps to the lectern to deliver a eulogy in Latin, recounting the highlights of his Pontiff's reign. The eulogy written on a scroll is then placed in a brass cylinder and deposited at the feet of the Pope, after which more ceremonial prayers are recited by the celebrants. As the service enters its final moments the Archpriest of the Basilica announces in an emotional voice that the Pontiff's remains are about to be placed into the first of three coffins by three of the cardinals who had been raised to the Sacred College by him.

The first coffin is of cypress. Into this are deposited a number of gold, silver and copper commemorative coins and medals struck during the deceased Pope's reign. This is for the purpose of aiding in the identification of the Pope's remains should there be an exhumation or a dispute at some future time.

Over the length of his body is placed a red ermine blanket to warm him in the vault. At this point twenty cardinals step forward to incense and to sprinkle the body with holy water.

After bolting the cypress wood coffin, the prelates then lower it, with red ropes, inside one of lead. This casket, emblazoned with the Pope's coat of arms, is also sealed and the two are then placed inside a plain coffin of elm. There is much symbolism to all this. The cypress tree represents death and has in Italy as far back as the Etruscan period; the lead symbolizes the hope of preservation; the elm demonstrates that the Pope, though Vicar of Christ on Earth, shares a common bond with humble men everywhere who are lowered into the earth in a wooden box.

When the clanking of hammers and the buzzing of drills which resounds through the immense church is finished, the triple coffin is covered with a purple pall. Here the Archpriest sadly chants: *Circumdederunt me gemitus mortis et doloris inferni, Domine.* (The sighs of death and the pains of hell surround me, O Lord.)

As the body is lowered through the well in front of the main altar into the grottoes below, the choir fills the sacred edifice with celestial song. A group of prelates escort the body to the tomb. There they recite the *Pater Noster,* bless the coffins and the crypt that the Pope had chosen early in his reign.

(Most Popes are buried in or near St. Peter's. Some, however, wished to sleep the eternal sleep in another favorite church. Pius IX for example reposes in the venerable Basilica of St. Lawrence Outside the Walls, Leo XIII in the Lateran Basilica of St. John.)

Gently the coffins are laid in the tomb, the tomb is sealed and another Pontificate has ended.

Now the attention of the City and the World turns to the coming *conclave,* the assembly of all the members of the College of Cardinals, which will create the next Pope. Newspapers of the Eternal City run biographical sketches of all the princes of the Church and lists of Papabili, the most "papable," that is to say, those with the best chances for election. From the great chariot racing days in the ancient Circus Maximus to our own era, Civis Romanus has had a weakness for a friendly wager or two. And so as the conclave draws nearer the betting grows more feverish in the bars and cafes across Rome as some proprietors even put up tote boards with the names of the papabili and the odds on each.

The system of conclaves or papal elections as we know it today took more than a millennium to evolve. We do not have a great deal of information about the election process in the earliest centuries. But what little we do have leads us to believe that the Bishop of Rome was chosen as was the bishop of any other see, i.e., by the diocesan clergy and laity. There is a letter extant written by Pope St. Clement in A.D. 98 to the Corinthians suggesting that this was the case. And we are told in a letter by St. Cyprian of Carthage in A.D. 251 of the election of Pope St. Cornelius to the Bishopric of the Roman See in the same manner.

We learn too that sometimes the Bishop of Rome, that is to say, of course, the Pope, would choose his successor with the advice and consent of the bishops of nearby sees. This practice could be considered an ancient forerunner of the conclave system. In the post-Constantine era Papal elections were often held in the Basilica of St. John Lateran, with the city's clergy and laity casting ballots.

When Popes became temporal rulers in the eighth century this system corrupted. For with so much political power at stake other rulers would be anxious for a Pope compatible with their interests and consequently they would seek to manipulate the elections.

As a result the elections were often accompanied by violence and bloodshed. Once, one aspirant to the Chair of Peter had been so incensed at his defeat that he and his backers went on a rampage, invading churches and slaughtering the faithful.

The election of 1059 had been a particularly stormy one. When the dust settled, Gerard of Burgundy, bishop of Florence and a good and holy man, was enthroned as Nicholas II. Scandalized by the secular and political interference with the election of the Supreme Pontiff of Mother Church, Pope Nicholas struck a major blow for reform with his new plan for the election of a Pope which he revealed to a synod of bishops held in Rome later that year. This courageous step taken toward Papal independence outraged many of the power brokers of Europe, especially those of the German court. Nicholas decreed that henceforth only the cardinal-bishops should elect the successor to Peter.

A century later Pope Alexander III, at the Third Lateran Council, extended suffrage to all the cardinals, not only those who were bishops.

Now on to Viterbo. When Pope Clement IV died in 1268 in Viterbo, a historic city two hours north from Rome on the consular Via Cassia, seventeen cardinals convened there to select his successor. This little group found itself divided into several factions, each determined to block the choice of the others. They would meet for stretches of days and weeks but always wind up deadlocked. Then they would adjourn and return to their dioceses for a time, come back to Viterbo and go through the motions again. While two and a half years passed in this shameful way the Church remained without a Supreme Pontiff. Viterbo's town fathers, clergy, and citizens became disgusted with the hopeless stalemate and took matters into their own hands. They sealed the cardinals into the Papal palace, locked them in *cum clave* (Latin for: "with a key" hence the word, conclave). Food was passed through rotating doors in to the cardinals, now otherwise totally shut off from the outside world. Days passed and the cardinals remained intransigent. When a reduction in the food supply to just a little bread and water failed to produce results, the town fathers ordered the roof torn off the palace and the stubborn electors exposed to the elements. This got results. Though the cardinals had by their self-serving ways caused the Church much distress, they redeemed themselves at least a little when they gave to the Church a great leader in Tedaldo Visconti, whom history remembers as Pope Blessed Gregory X.

Resolved that the Church should never again go through another such an endless *Sede Vacante,* Gregory laid down these rules:

1. When a Pontiff dies the cardinals will celebrate funeral rites for nine days. On the tenth day they will

lock themselves up in the residence of the dead Pope. Each will be allowed to bring two aides with him.

2. There shall be no access to the cardinals from the outside world for the duration of the conclave.

3. A few windows shall be left open through which food may be passed.

4. After three days of deliberations, the cardinals' diet shall be cut to one dish per meal, and after eight days to bread and water.

5. All ecclesiastical and legal offices of the Papal Court shall be suspended during the interregnum.

6. The cardinals will confine their activity and their attention—except for a Church emergency—to the election of a successor to the Chair of Peter.

7. If a cardinal does not enter the conclave, or leaves before it is concluded, the election is to go on without him.

8. For election two-thirds of all votes cast shall be required.

9. If a Pope dies outside the city where he had resided, the cardinals, if possible, will meet in the city of the Pope's death.

10. Officials of the city of the conclave will see that all of these laws governing the conclave are observed.

11. These officials shall swear an oath that they will do so.

12. Failing this, said officials shall be excommunicated.

13. With regard to the election, the cardinals shall disregard their personal interests and think only of the common good of the Church.

14. None of the electors shall seek the office nor campaign on anyone else's behalf.

15. In all cities of importance solemn memorial ceremonies will be celebrated upon the death of a Pope, and public prayers offered every day for the swift election of a new and good successor.

These laws promulgated in 1274 still obtain with the exception of a few details. Some of the regulations have been eased but to this day the basic concept of the cardinals' absolute separation from the secular world is still in effect.

The spread of the Church across the Atlantic to North America in later centuries would cause some problems with the first regulation of Gregory X, i.e., that the cardinals convene within ten days. In 1914 after the death of Pope St. Pius X, Cardinal O'Connell of Boston sailed across the vast ocean and arrived in Rome one hour after the cardinals had chosen Giacomo della Chiesa to succeed to the Pontificate as Benedict XV. Eight years later, O'Connell, sailing on the fastest boat of the time, was visibly upset when upon his arrival in Rome he was told that another election was over. The new Pope, Pius XI, rushed to embrace the frustrated American prelate and express his personal regrets along with his assurances that this would never happen again. One of the first measures of the new Pontificate was a revision of the regulation from ten to fifteen days with an option of a three day extension to provide enough time for cardinals coming from far-off places. Ironically swift transoceanic flights which were just around the corner were soon to render the revision quite unnecessary. Today with our rapid communications and nonstop European flights an American prince of the Church could be in the Eternal City within hours of a Pontiff's passing. (Incidentally, Cardinal O'Connell finally got the privilege to cast a vote in the 1939 conclave which elected Eugenio Pacelli.)

Another departure from Gregory X's guidelines is that in recent centuries the Sistine Chapel has been the site of Papal elections.

Originally the conclave was but one large room where the cardinals would spend all their time, deliberating there, eating there, even sleeping there. Now it encompasses an entire section of the Apostolic Palace which is walled off via temporary partitions from the rest of the palace complex. Today when a conclave is called, legions of Vatican carpenters erect partitions

The Basilica of St. Peter, largest Church in all of Christendom and major landmark of Vatican City.

A cross crowns the bronze baldacchino—work of the Baroque genius, Bernini—over the high altar of St. Peter's.

Left: View—from the papal gardens—of Michelangelo's soaring cupola.

Part of the colonnades, by Bernini, that embrace the vast Square of St. Peter. The Square is called by some "The Vatican's Lobby." Also in the scene is one of the twin fountains that grace the piazza, this one by Stefano Maderno, who also designed the facade of the basilica.

Right: Bernini's bronze chair of St. Peter which contains the wooden chair that tradition says was used by St. Peter.

The bronze baldacchino, or canopy, above the Confession or Tomb of St. Peter. With its twisted columns representing the energy and vitality of the Church, the canopy, constructed of bronze taken from the roof of the Pantheon, rises to the height of a ten-story building.

Left: Bronze statue of St. Peter, clutching the keys, with its right foot worn smooth by the touches and kisses of pilgrims across the centuries.

Facade of St. John Lateran, the cathedral of the Diocese of Rome. The Lateran property, gift of Constantine to the Christian community, enjoys today extra-territorial Vatican status.

The Papal Altar of St. John Lateran. In the reliquary above the altar are the heads of the apostles, Peter and Paul. The Pope, in his capacity as Bishop of Rome, has St. John's as his cathedral.

The patriarchal basilica of St. Paul's-Outside-The-Walls. About a mile beyond the city walls, the basilica, commissioned by Constantine in 326, rises over the tomb of Paul the Apostle.

To the right of the main altar, the statue of Paul. With his sword in one hand, a book in the other, Paul is portrayed as Christianity's most vigorous defender and most learned scholar.

View, from the Papal Altar to the main entrance, of the interior of St. Paul's.

Facade of St. Mary Major, one of the four patriarchal basilicas. It was commissioned by Pope Liberius in the 4th century.

Central aisle of St. Mary Major.

Top left: A Swiss guard on duty near one of the
entrances to the Vatican. Top right: Author presents his
credentials to guard, Reto Murer. In background, the
Vatican State flag.

Bottom: The tiny, colorfully-clad army marches into
St. Peter's Square for the Pope's Easter Mass.

Twelve noon, Sunday. The Holy Father greets the crowd in the square. From his window on the top floor of the Apostolic Palace, the Pontiff imparts his bene-diction, while the great bells of St. Peter's ring out joyously.

The Sistine Room (commissioned by Pope Sixtus V, 1585-1590) of the Vatican Library with its precious
ancient manuscripts on display in glass cases and its walls adorned by Renaissance frescoes.

The Gallery of Busts, in the Chiaramonti wing of the Vatican Museum.

Fountain of the Eagle in the sprawling Papal Gardens.

The Casina of Pius IV in the gardens. The work of Pirro Ligorio, this delicate structure served Pius (1558-1562) as his summer villa. Today it serves as the seat of the Pontifical Academy of Sciences.

PIVS SEXTVS P M
TEVTONVM ET FLANDROR
COEMETERIVM
IN ELEGANTIOREM CVLTVM
RESTITVIT A PONTIF IV

Author pauses to read the Latin inscription over the gate to the Vatican's Teutonic Cemetery.

Top: Author studies a 3rd century sarcophagus in the Catacombs of St. Callistus on the Appian Way.

Bottom: Tomb painting in the catacombs, showing a Eucharistic rite.

The Colosseum, mightiest symbol of pagan Rome, where, tradition tells us, countless thousands of Christians suffered martyrdom. On Good Friday evening, the Pope, carrying a huge wooden cross, leads a candlelight procession to the arena to commemorate the suffering of the early Christians.

Left: The Mamertine Prison's Tullianum dungeon where Peter and Paul were incarcerated.

Interior of the ancient stadium, showing the elaborate subterranean network of storage rooms, gladiator quarters, animal cells.

Right: Forum Magnum, *the great Forum, seat of the anti-Christian government of Imperial Rome.*

Castel Sant'Angelo (Hadrian's Tomb) on the banks of the Tiber. In previous centuries it served as a Papal citadel.

San Paolo alle Tre Fontane—St. Paul's at the Three Fountains. Charming little 5th century church built on the spot where St. Paul was beheaded.

Top and Bottom: The interior of the Church of St. Paul at the Three Fountains.

Frank Korn—in left corner of photo—listens intently to the Holy Father's remarks at a summer Sunday audience in Castel Gandolfo.

Pius XII

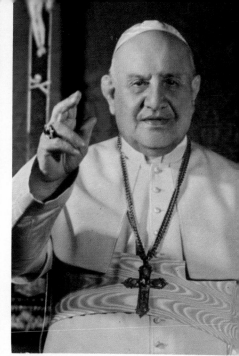

John XXIII

Paul VI

Top: John Paul I strolls in the Vatican Gardens.
Bottom: John Paul II attending to one of his favorite
duties—mingling with his spiritual children.

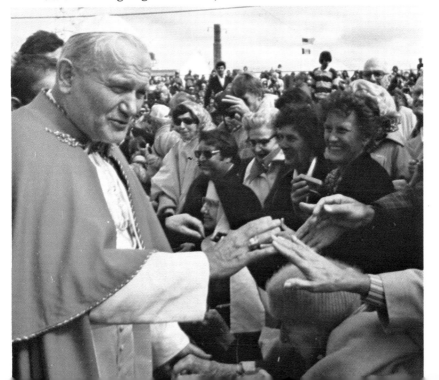

The little balcony at the top of the dome of St. Peter's affords this sweeping view of Eternal Rome.

subdividing rooms, antechambers, hallways to create cells for the cardinals and their two-man staffs. Cooks, waiters, electricians, plumbers, guards, doctors, barbers, general handymen are assigned to the conclave for its duration. Meals are taken in a common refectory. The cells, monastic in size and trappings, are given just a touch of esthetics with a covering of green cloth. Each is equipped with a bed, a writing table, a few chairs, a kneeling bench, a washstand and metal basin and a clothes rack. On the wall behind the bed is a crucifix.

There is but one door to the conclave. Today, through the courtyard of St. Damasus. Once the electoral assembly officially commences, that door is locked and remains so until the conclusion of the election. To ensure further against outside influences, all windows of the conclave area are boarded up and all glass doors painted over. Telephone lines are cut off. The government of the conclave resides in the hands of the Camerlengo.

On the morning of the day the conclave is to begin the cardinals gather for a Mass of the Holy Spirit at which they pray for divine guidance in their solemn task. Then they return to their cells or visit colleagues or tend to some pressing personal matter, not knowing how long they will be confined starting that same evening.

At about four in the afternoon conclave officials perform an ancient rite, roaming through the pertinent areas of the Apostolic palace searching for unauthorized persons. As they search one aide continues to call out in Latin: "Exeant Omnes!" (Everyone must leave!)

An hour later the conclave officially begins and the cardinals move in formal procession to the Sistine Chapel to chant the *Veni Creator Spiritus,* once again imploring God's guidance.

The brief service closes with the cardinals swearing an oath of secrecy in the deliberations. There is no voting on the first day. The cardinals pass the rest of the evening dining, visiting one another, walking in the courtyards, praying, meditating, reading.

Dawn breaks over Rome on the second day of the conclave as the city grows increasingly anxious to learn who will become the next bishop of the Petrine See. At about seven o'clock that morning attendants pass through the corridors knocking on cell doors exclaiming: *"In cappelam, Domini!"* (Into the chapel, Lords!) Soon the cardinals gather for a procession into the Pauline Chapel (named for Pope Paul III) at eight for Mass. Following this rite the cardinals repair to the dining area for the light traditional Roman breakfast of a roll, a little juice, and a cup of *caffe e' latte.* From here they repair to their cells to be helped into the ritual violet robes of the conclave. By nine-thirty they begin to assemble again and precisely at ten the impressive procession into the Sistine begins. Accompanying the cardinals at this point are their aides bearing portfolios. The Papal princes then take their respective places on individual thrones lining both side walls. A canopy extends out over each throne. The canopies symbolize that when there is no Pope the members of the Sacred College are supreme in the Church hierarchy. Before each throne is a small writing desk equipped with a sort of scorecard to enable each elector to tabulate the returns as they are read aloud by the *scrutatores,* or counters, seated before the main altar.

Upon that altar stand six tall lighted candles and a large chalice which will serve as a ballot box. High up on the ceiling Michelangelo's Old Testament giants now gaze down upon a polling place.

Nearby is a cloak room where the Vatican tailors have prepared white vestments for the new Holy Father in three different sizes; small, medium, and large. In another room off the chapel is a small black stove with a pipe extending up into a chimney pipe above the Sistine Chapel. It is this pipe which by the color of its smoke communicates to Rome and to the universe whether or not a vote has been conclusive. About this I will have more to say shortly.

According to Church custom the election can take place in three ways: inspiration, compromise, or secret ballot. The third method is, of course, by far the most common.

Inspiration takes place when, miraculously, the cardinals are moved by the Holy Spirit to proclaim, spontaneously and unanimously, someone to be Supreme Pontiff. Compromise occurs when the Cardinals are hopelessly deadlocked and entrust the election to a committee of three or five or seven of their membership. In this method there must be unanimity among the committee members for election.

Who may be elected? Any baptized Catholic male may in theory succeed to the Throne of Peter but in practice, for many centuries now, the new Vicar of Christ comes from among the cardinals. Remember that there are three orders of cardinal: Cardinal-Bishop, Cardinal-Priest, Cardinal-Deacon. The ranking member of each order along with the Camerlengo conduct the electoral proceedings. When the ballots are about to be distributed, all but the cardinals themselves must leave the polling area, i.e., the Sistine Chapel. Prayers are offered before the altar by the conclave conductors and then each elector receives a ballot worded this way:

Ego, Cardinalis _____,   Eligo
In Summum Pontificem Reverendissimum
Dominum Meum, Dominum Cardinalem _____.

(I, Cardinal _____,   Elect
To the Supreme Pontificate, My Most
Reverend Lord, Lord Cardinal _____.)

In the first blank each elector enters his name and in the second the name of his choice. For further identification, in the event of a disputed ballot, the voter writes a scriptural text on the bottom portion of the ballot. And in a further attempt at secrecy each cardinal makes an effort to disguise his handwriting.

To serve as tabulators three cardinals have been chosen by lot. After the electors finish marking their papers they proceed, in order of seniority, to the altar.

Each holds his ballot with two fingers of the right hand. At the altar he kneels, prays, and then swears this oath: "I call to witness, Christ, Our Lord and Our Judge, that I have chosen him whom I think should be elected according to the will of God."

Then he rises and deposits his ballot into the large chalice, genuflects before the crucifix, and returns to his canopied throne.

Should a cardinal be ill and confined to his cell the cardinals conducting the proceedings take a box with a slit in its top to the bedside so that he may still participate in the election.

When all have voted the three tabulators read each ballot, the first two to themselves, the third aloud. On the printed form in front of him every cardinal keeps his own tally. If, when the reading is over, there is not the same number of ballots as there are cardinals in the chamber, the vote is invalidated, all the papers burned, and another vote taken immediately.

All this while St. Peter's Square is filling up and overflowing with humanity. All eyes are fixed on the Sistine chimney pipe watching for the *fumata,* the few puffs of smoke which by their color will reveal whether or not the cardinals have reached a decision and given the Church a new Pontifex Maximus.

This is how it works. If in a balloting a two-thirds-plus-one majority has not been obtained by anyone, a second vote follows immediately. If this too proves inconclusive, all the ballots of both votes are put in the black stove mentioned earlier. Some damp straw and a little pitch are added so that when the ballots are burned a black smoke is given off. When the throngs in the square see the dark emission they groan in disappointment and slowly break up. They will be back faithfully for the next voting session and hope again to be witnesses to history.

On the other hand when a Pope has been chosen, only the ballots are burnt, causing a whitish smoke to emanate from the slender smokestack, in turn causing an indescribable uproar of joy in *Piazza San Pietro.*

When a cardinal has received a sufficient number of votes the dean of the Sacred College proceeds to the throne of the Pope-elect and addresses this question to him: *"Acceptasne electionem de te canonice factam in Summan Pontificem?"* (Do you accept your election, carried out according to the law, to the Supreme Pontificate?)

One Latin word in response is all that is required to end the Sede Vacante: *"Accepto."* (I accept.) Once the elected one utters that word the Church has a new Holy Father. His coronation some days later will be but a beautiful, imposing, fitting ceremony to mark another great milestone in Church history.

The Pope is elected for life. If he should choose to resign, which is his privilege but one which is almost never exercised, another conclave will be summoned.

After the word *"accepto"* has been spoken, the cardinals flock to their new Father to wish him well and to pledge their loyalty.

Various Popes have reacted in various ways upon election. We are told that Giuseppe Sarto (Pius X) was visibly shaken and frightened and very reluctantly uttered the fateful word. At one point when his election seemed inevitable he had tried to dissuade the cardinals from choosing him, tearfully insisting that he was unworthy and incapable. Little Giacomo Della Chiesa (Benedict XV) viewed his election as God's plan and calmly and confidently accepted. Eugenio Pacelli is reported to have buried his head in his hands murmuring again and again: "Miserere mei, Deus." (Have pity on me, Lord.) Calm resignation to the will of God manifested through the will of the cardinals was Roncalli's reaction, but his successor, Montini, was almost as terrified as was Sarto. Way back in 440 Pope Saint Leo had cried regarding his election: "A burden to shudder at."

When the cardinals are done with their felicitations, the formalities resume. The dean of the Sacred College asks the new Pontiff: "Quo nomine vis vocari?" (By what name do you wish to be called?) His Holiness reveals his choice of a Pontifical name and then usually makes a short statement explaining his choice. Pacelli explained that he wished to be called Pius because "most of my life has been spent during the reign of a Pope by that name and because of my grateful memory of Pius XI, who showed such love for me." For many centuries Popes have upon election changed their names in memory of the fact that Christ when making Simon Bar-Jonah the first head of His Church changed his name to Peter.

The Pontiff now proceeds to the sacristy to vest himself in one of the three waiting white cassocks. He also dons a red stole and puts a red mantle around his shoulders. Vested in the garments of his new office, the Pope, who from this time on will sign all his documents P.P. (Papa Pontifex) or *Servus Servorum Dei* (Servant of the Servants of God), returns to the Sistine where a throne is waiting for him at the altar. Each cardinal comes forward to kneel before the successor of Simon Bar-Jonah and to kiss his foot and his hand symbolizing the supremacy of Peter.

Outside all this time the frantic crowd, having seen the *fumata bianca* (white smoke) nearly an hour ago, waits in heart-pounding anticipation of its first glimpse of the next Bishop of Rome. After the long period of solemnity there is now a brief interlude of levity as the windows of the Vatican Palace and of the corridors leading to the Basilica are opened and at them appear many of the conclavists waving happily to the people. At the election of Pius X one of the conclavists appeared at a window and using his fingers as scissors made a gesture, several times, of cutting cloth. Perceptive Italians in the square knew at once who their new Pope was. It was the tailor! (Sarto means tailor in Italian and this must have sent many of them scurrying to place some last minute *Papabili* bets at the cafes near Saint Peter's.)

Though events are and have been moving rapidly inside the conclave ever since the decisive vote, the minutes are months to the waiting Romans and tourists locked in the embrace of Bernini's colonnade. But it shan't be long now, for the Pope is at the moment on his way to the central outer balcony to be introduced to an anxious world.

Suddenly the glass doors of the balcony are thrown open and Vatican servants lower over the railing a huge tapestry of the coat of arms of the last Pope. The noise in the square crescendoes and crashes against Maderno's iron-gray facade. Minutes later the ranking cardinal deacon appears and within an instant the pandemonium miraculously metamorphoses into a fragile silence.

Another eternal minute passes with the sound of shuffling papers on the lectern, picked up by the sensitive microphones, the only violation of the silence. Then the cardinal begins the long-awaited Latin proclamation:

Nuntio vobis magnum gaudium! (I announce to you a great joy!) A murmur ripples through the crowd. *Habemus Papam!* (We have a Pope!) The murmur increases and in a moment all is still again. *Reverendissimum Dominum, Dominum Cardinalem Montini!* (The most reverend Lord, Lord Cardinal Montini!) Pandemonium reigns once more. Then one last part to the announcement: *Qui sibi nomen imposuit, Paulus Sextus!* (Who has taken the name, Paul the Sixth!)

The people exult, church bells across Rome resound. Some in the crowd begin a rhythmic clapping, calling for the new Pope to appear which he will do in just moments. Cries of *Viva Il Papa!* explode in the clear Mediterranean air. And then suddenly and magically a slim figure in white and red appears on the balcony to receive the welcoming ovation from his urban and universal flock. Some weep from joy, some embrace, some bless themselves, some wave frantically, some kneel in thanksgiving, all are deeply moved.

When there is sufficient calm the new Holy Father raises his right hand and begins the sign of the cross, imparting his first *Urbi et Orbi* (to the City and to the

World) blessing: *"In nomine Patris, et Filii, et Spiritus Sancti."* The crowd *una voce* (with one voice) chants: *"Amen."*

Then the Pontiff with his arms open, his palms facing heaven, stands there a while to accept the thunderous applause which is punctuated by more cries of *"Viva Il Papa!"* And suddenly he is gone, back to the Apostolic Palace to plunge full steam into his incredible task.

Far into the night some of the people still mill around in the darkened square reluctant to bring to a close perhaps the most memorable day in their lives. Another pontificate has begun.

A week or so after this thrilling day, Rome is in a festive mood once more for the beautiful installation ceremonies. Until Pope John Paul I decided against it the ceremony used to be one of coronation, in the Basilica. Though we shall probably never see one again, a Papal Coronation used to be a strikingly beautiful and symbolic ritual that I should like to describe for you briefly: Eighty-five thousand people would fill every cubic inch of St. Peter's floor to watch the centuries of tradition unfold. Silver trumpets blared from the inside balcony of the dome, signaling the start of the ceremonies. The main doors swung open and through them flowed a brilliant procession of guards and knights in dazzling uniforms, the diplomatic corps and members of the Papal Court, clerics in black, monks in brown, bishops in violet, cardinals in flaming red. At the end of this endless line was borne the Holy Father on the *Sedia gestatoria* carried on the shoulders of twelve *sediarii*. After the people had given another tumultuous greeting to the Pope, now robed in white, gold-brocaded vestments, a bejeweled stole, and a gold miter the Sistine Choir would chant the Papal hymn, *Tu Es Petrus.* Then the Pontiff followed the colorful river of ecclesiastical vestments down the main aisle.

Lest this majestic show turn his head, the Church provided an admonition to the Pontiff. Walking backwards before the Pope's portable throne was the Master of Ceremonies carrying a small burner and a handful of flax. One third of the way down the aisle the procession halted and the Pope took some flax and dropped it into the burner whereupon it disappeared in an instant of flame and smoke. The Master of Ceremonies then called out solemnly: *"Sancte Pater, Sic Transit Gloria Mundi!"* (Holy Father, thus passes the glory of the world!) Two thirds of the way down the aisle, this fascinating vignette would be repeated, and once more before the main altar to remind the Pope that all earthly glory is fleeting, that he, like the rest of us, is here on earth not for self aggrandizement but for the greater honor and glory of God and the chance to be with Him in Paradise.

At the end of the aisle the Pope would leave the sedia and ascend the throne near the main altar. Here again the cardinals would come forward to pay tribute and pledge obedience. Then he climbed the steps to the altar beneath Bernini's bronze canopy of twisted columns to celebrate his first Pontifical Mass over the tomb of the first Pope. The Epistle and Gospel were sung in both Latin and Greek to symbolize the unity of East and West in the Catholic Church. The liturgy was elaborate and wondrous to behold. When the Pope pronounced the words *Sanctus, Sanctus, Sanctus, Dominus Deus....* (Holy, Holy, Holy is the Lord God...) all knelt. Eight cardinals assisting at the Mass held lighted torches before the altar. Moments later His Holiness consecrated the bread and wine, transubtantiating it into the Body and Blood of his Divine Master. He elevated the Host and then the chalice while the twelve trumpeters in the dome filled the hall with the sacred hymn "Largo" by the eighteenth century composer Longhi.

Just before the Communion, the Pope embraced the cardinals assisting him in the Kiss of Peace. Then before taking Communion under both species, Body and Blood, he pronounced the words: *"Domine, non sum dignus"* (Lord, I am not worthy...).

When the Mass ended, the Pope remounted the sedia and the procession regrouped to escort him back out of the basilica, through the immense bronze doors and up the Scala Regia, the Palace staircase, that leads to the huge balcony facing St. Peter's Square.

Shortly, the Holy Father was facing Rome again, the multitude now spilling down into the Via della Conciliazione. This time, in a spontaneous expression of love and joy, many would wave something, a kerchief, a hat, a little flag. The Pope then imparted his Apostolic Blessing left and right.

With the crowning about to take place, the Pontiff would seat himself on a gilded throne. A cardinal stepped forward and took the golden miter, the high-pointed ceremonial hat of a bishop, from the Pope's head. The senior cardinal deacon then lifted the jeweled tiara from the red velvet little cushion it had been carried on throughout the day and placed it, as an emblem of the Pope's sovereignty, upon the Holy Father's head, saying: Receive the tiara, adorned with three crowns, and know that thou art the Father of Princes and Kings, Rector of the Universe, Vicar of Our Savior, Jesus Christ.

The coronation was over. The Pope rose to impart his benediction again. He returned to his holy work and Rome to the status quo.

Each of the last two Pontiffs has shied away from a coronation, however, and even a less ritualistic enthronement, in favor of a simple outdoor Mass to mark the beginning of his mission as Supreme Pastor. This is altogether appropriate since the days when the Holy Father was also truly a temporal ruler are long since passed.

6

A Day With the Vatican's Head of State

In this chapter let us go behind the scenes of the Vatican for twenty-four hours to watch the Holy Father at work. It is one of my hopes here at least to dispel some misconceptions about the Pontiff's typical day and general lifestyle.

Back in the States I teach some college courses in Roman Civilization. One day a few years ago in class we got into a discussion of the early Christian community in Rome, which led to a discussion of the early Papacy, which in turn swept us along through the middle ages and eventually and inevitably to an exchange about the modern Pontificate. One otherwise well-informed young student caustically observed that the Pope lives monarchically in a palace ornamented in precious works of art, that he travels about in a golden jet and his lavish yachts, that he possesses tons of precious jewelry and gorges himself at lucullan banquets each evening while half the world is starving and in rags. Let us now clarify things a bit.

The Vatican is a tiny country which my sons, their mom, and I have walked from border to border many times, a journey of perhaps fifteen minutes. It is not even the size of a good-sized golf course, and it is cluttered with so many huge buildings that indeed one would be hard put to land a toy airplane anywhere in the Pope's "country." The notion of Papal yachts is just as absurd when one considers that the largest body of water in the Vatican City State is a basin a few meters in length and width that catches the cascading waters of one of the fountains in the Vatican Gardens.

A palace? Yes, but only a small portion of one floor is used for the Papal apartment. The rest of the complex is for various offices of the Church administration. Works of art? Yes, in the wing of the Apostolic Palace that serves as a museum and which is open to all the people of the world to enjoy.

The Holy Father has a couple of episcopal rings and pectoral crosses for his entire jewelry collection and these have a material value of perhaps twenty dollars each.

Despite his lofty and sacred office the Pope lives an almost monastic private life. The Pope's apartment is free of all luxury. His bedroom is outfitted with a plain bed, a night table, a prie dieu, a soft chair, and a wooden crucifix on the wall opposite the bed. A walnut table, a few ordinary chairs, two wooden cupboards constitute the trappings of his dining room. And particularly meager is the Holy Father's wardrobe: a few white cassocks of different weights for the changing seasons, a topcoat and a couple of skullcaps (zucchettos), also white, some pairs of red velvet shoes and two red shoulder capes. One could scarcely count as part of the Pope's wardrobe the various ceremonial vestments and miters used for the celebration of solemn Pontifical rites.

The Pope's private study is modest too, consisting chiefly of a desk cluttered with an endless and merciless supply of work to be done each day.

His diet is also modest. Indeed in his eating habits the Holy Father, and many of his predecessors, could accurately be described as ascetic. And like many of those who bore the Keys before him, John Paul II practices self-denial and mortification. To increase his personal sanctity he spends many of his precious few private moments each day on his knees in prayer.

Pius XII was known to have slept on the floor. St. Pius X and John XXIII were known to have given away to the needy all personal monetary property as quickly as they came into it. Paul VI wore a hair shirt. All went to their grave, as will John Paul II, penniless.

The only luxury the Pope might enjoy in his private life is domestic help, and this is so only that he might be all the more free to cope with the incomparable, indescribable, incredible task of running the world-wide institution of Mother Church. Throughout the Vatican and to points in or near Rome the Pope is chauffered in a Mercedes donated to the Holy See by the car's manufacturer.

But my ill-informed student's allegations notwithstanding, be assured that the Vatican does not have, nor does it have any plans for, either an airport or a harbor.

Day breaks in the Italian region of Lazio and the sun peers over the rugged shoulders of the Alban Hills, and, climbing higher every minute, it begins to illuminate the pastel shades of Rome's old buildings, the aged travertine of her fountains and churches and palaces, the verdant loveliness of her pines, and cypresses, and ilexes. Thousands upon thousands of wooden shutters on both sides of the lethargic Tiber open on another entry in the city's eternal diary.

At the same time, behind the Vatican walls, the curtain is rising for the next scene in the long and solemn drama of the Papacy. Rising with the sun, and that curtain, is Pope John Paul II, Vicar of Christ on Earth, to face another eighteen to twenty-hour day in the vineyards of his Divine Master. Today as on all days he will wrestle with a host of problems in all his capacities as Bishop of Rome, Sovereign of Vatican City State, Supreme Pastor of the Universal Church, Fisherman of Souls, Spiritual Father of the world's Catholics. John Paul begins each day, in his sandstone colored bedroom on the top floor of the Apostolic Palace, on his knees at the prie dieu beneath the wooden crucifix, thanking God for the chance to serve Him with all his heart and soul, mind and body, for still another day.

Having completed his prayers, His Holiness—the azure eyes already alert, the wispy white hair falling over his rugged forehead, the burly, slightly round-shouldered frame ready for the day's burdens—strides over to the window to peek through the slats of the shutters for a quick weather check. The golden glory of a Mediterranean sunrise evokes a beaming smile that sends ripples across the broad planes of the handsome Slovak face. Then, the bath having been drawn by his faithful valet-chauffeur, Pope John Paul indulges his fondness for a hot tub, all the while sorting out his ideas for the day's work. Following this relaxing treat, the Holy Father shaves with an electric razor.

(A predecessor of his, Pius XII, also used an electric razor. But when he did each morning it would cause quite a stir in the Papal household. Let me explain. Pius loved birds and kept a number of them in his apartment. In fact, he had a Francis of Assisi-like rapport with all creatures. A favorite picture of mine is Pius, the Pope of my Catholic boyhood, cradling a lamb in his long and loving slender arms, smiling radiantly. Well, his favorite among the birds was Gretel, a spirited goldfinch who had a mad crush on the Holy Father and could not take her eyes off him. She would perch on his shoulder while he ate or wrote or conversed or prayed. When she heard the buzz of the razor each dawn she would shake herself awake, chirp excitedly, leap onto the little machine and ride it up and down the Pontifical face. At that precise moment they were probably the only two creatures stirring in the entire country [i.e., the Vatican]. For Pius XII, too, rose extremely early.)

(John Paul II's daily regimen is quite like that of Pius XII and as a matter of fact both in turn would compare very closely with those of all other Popes of this century.)

Now Pope John Paul II dons his everyday attire, a white tunic or cassock derived from the *tunica alba* of classical times. Made of white linen, the garment reaches to the feet, usually buttons down the front, is closefitting with tight long sleeves, and is belted with a wide, white, watermarked sash, that hangs down the left front side. At the bottom of the sash is a gold-embroidered papal seal. A small collarless white cape, the *mozzetta,* covers the shoulders and upper arms to the elbow. The Pontiff's stockings are white, his shoes (of leather or velvet) red. Against the stark white of the cassock is the Pope's pectoral cross, which contains a relic of the true cross. On the third finger of his left hand, the Holy Father wears the Fisherman's Ring, symbol of his succession to the Chair of Peter, the fisherman from Galilee. When it is chilly, the Pope will wear over his cassock a long cloak of red wool, the mantello. When he is completely vested, John Paul II places the small white *zucchetto* on his head, and opens the door to the corridor outside his bedroom where his personal aide, Father Stanislaw Dziwisz, is waiting. Together they head quietly for the Pope's small private chapel down the hall. With the bright rays by now streaming through the little stained-glass windows, the Pontiff begins his Mass, in Latin: *"In nomine Patris, et Filii, et Spiritus Sancti...."*

Following the Pope's Divine Service, Father Dziwisz offers his daily Mass, which the Pope hears from a side kneeling bench. When the priest's Mass is ended, the two recite together parts of their daily office, then for another half hour or so they devote themselves to silent prayer and meditation.

In the meantime, a couple of the five Polish nuns (of the order of the Sister Servants of the Sacred Heart) which keep the Papal household have been preparing breakfast. Unlike the skimpy continental breakfast of coffee and a roll which his Italian predecessors almost always opted for, the morning fare of the athletic Karol Wojtyla is somewhat substantial, and the delightful aromas that come from grilled sausage or ham and eggs, toasted homemade bread, and fresh-brewed coffee waft through the Pontifical chambers. (Much of the food for the Pope's table, especially the dairy products, is brought in fresh each day from the little farm of the

Papal summer villa out in the Alban Hills.) Still, the Holy Father takes relatively small portions.

The household duties of the Papal apartment are traditionally entrusted to a small team of nuns, though Papa Sarto, Pius X, gave that privilege to his three spinster sisters. Pope Pius XII's household was under the strict management of a tough little Bavarian nun, Sister Pasqualina, who first came into the Holy Father's service when he was Papal Nuncio to Berlin and who remained with him to his death. She had received a single, simple, but serious mandate from the Pontiff, to wit: "Look after my health, so I can forget about it." She took him literally and determined his diet, his workload, his company. Sister Pasqualina thought nothing of barging in on a lengthy meeting of the Pope with his aides, or with cardinals, or even with foreign dignitaries and telling all the visitors *via, per favore!* (Please leave!) *La Sua Santita è stanco!* (His Holiness is tired!) Pius would usually grin wryly and apologetically explain: "Sister Pasqualina knows what is best for us."

Pope John Paul and his aide get back from chapel sometime near eight o'clock and take breakfast together. (For centuries, popes had traditionally dined alone. John XXIII, an incurable extrovert, however, tried this for about a week into his reign and found it depressing. He then began to invite others to share meals with him, pointing out: "I have searched the Scriptures and nowhere do they say that the Pope must dine alone.") Following the light *colazione* the two men sit around the table and speed-read a couple of dozen of Europe's leading daily newspapers. This is the Pope's way of staying *au courant* with international issues and developments, and with public sentiment toward him and his reign. After perhaps a half hour of scanning, John Paul II and Father Stanislaw repair to the Pope's study to confer about the day's many appointments and about the matters His Holiness will be taking up with the heads of the various Curia departments.

Toward mid-morning Pope John Paul makes his way down, via elevator, to the official Papal office on the second floor. This room is actually his library and is alternately referred to as the *Biblioteca Privata.* An elegantly appointed room with shelves of books from floor to ceiling on three walls, it has three large windows which afford a glorious view of St. Peter's Square with its Egyptian obelisk, Baroque fountains, and open-mouthed tourists. Here is where the Pope usually receives important visitors to the Vatican.

The first one in to see the Holy Father in the *Biblioteca* each morning is usually the Vatican Secretary of State, Agostino Cardinal Casaroli. The scholarly and personable Casaroli engages in a conversation with the Pontiff which might well treat matters concerning every corner of the earth. A typical wide-ranging colloquy between the Pope and his chief representative might focus on recent unrest in a small African nation and the ramifications for Catholic religious there, on Arab terrorism around the Mediterranean, on the problems of the missions in Latin America, on the need for more bishops in North America, on Archbishop La Febvre and his unauthorized seminary and his persistence in celebrating Mass in the obsolete Tridentine rite, on the hostage crisis in Iran, on the claims of an apparition in some European backwater village, on a number of beatification and canonization causes, etc., etc., etc., *ad infinitum.*

From this taxing meeting, Pope John Paul then proceeds through a number of antechambers on the same floor where small groups (each numbering anywhere from four to fifteen or twenty persons) await a semi-private audience with the Holy Father. Private audiences are usually granted only to heads of state or their highest representatives.

(My family and I, having been part-time residents of Rome throughout most of Pope Paul VI's reign, were privileged to participate in a number of these small gatherings with *Papa Montini,* as the Romans affectionately called Paul VI. In the late sixties we used to remark on how he strode so briskly and vigorously into the room and on his militarily-erect Lombard frame. In

the early seventies we used to worry how he was beginning to slow down. In the late seventies we would fight
back tears when we witnessed the painful effort he had
to make to walk at all.)

Each Pope has demonstrated an individual style in
these audiences. John XXIII used to like to inject humor
and informality to put his guests at ease. He would, for
example, sometimes shock the Vatican protocol people
by even walking the last group to the elevator. Never
could he understand the fuss over this. "This is my
house and I was simply showing some guests to the
door." One day an American congressman, Brooks
Hayes, wanting to say something appropriate, nervously blurted out when the Pope approached him: "I'm
a Baptist." His Holiness grinned sympathetically and
retorted: "What a happy coincidence! I'm John!"

Pius XII, by nature very shy and contemplative, was
particularly buoyant and fatherly at these meetings
which he enjoyed thoroughly and looked forward to
eagerly. Once a wounded soldier dropped one of his
crutches and the Holy Father bent quickly to pick it up
for him. On another occasion an elderly lady asked if he
might hear her confession. To the astonishment of all,
Pius took her off to a corner and heard the signora's sins
and gave her absolution. Pius also had one of his aides
follow him with a box of medals and rosaries and, circumstances allowing, he would turn, reach into the box
and give everyone a tangible memento of his or her
meeting with the Holy Father.

Pope St. Pius X also enjoyed meeting his people in
this format and through these audiences he was often
credited with all types of miracles. A German gentle-
man, blind from birth, claimed the gift of sight had come
to him the instant that Pope Pius X made the Sign of the
Cross on his eyes. A lame boy, at Pius' exhortation, got
up and walked across the room to his parents. One
young lady managed to secure one of the Pope's socks
—perhaps from one of the Holy Father's sisters who
served as his housekeepers—and gave it to a friend with
a painful crippled foot. Upon putting on the sock the

friend was cured of her affliction. The humble and some-what embarrassed Pope tried to play all this down, sometimes with self-deprecating humor. "My feet ache all the time and my socks never seem to help them," he joked when informed of his latest "miracle."

To the very end Pope Paul VI struggled, even in such small groups and even after sixteen years in the Pontificate, with a lifelong shyness and natural reserve. The inveterate scholar, with his marvelously cultivated mind, accustomed to the rarefied air of theology, philosophy, doctrine and literature found it a problem to make small talk and exchange simple amenities. Nonetheless he did very well at it and was enormously popular with all who were fortunate enough to meet him that way.

Il Papa del Sorriso (the Pope with the Smile), John Paul I, delighted all his visitors with his informality. In fact his reign—tragically too brief to produce any encyclicals, reforms, or travels—is largely and dearly remembered for his audiences at which he was wont to spin homespun yarns to make a moral or theological point and to lovingly quiz children on their catechism lessons.

John Paul II obviously relishes these daily contacts with his spiritual children and his audiences too are characterized by a pleasant informality. He will storm vigorously into a chamber and put all of the wide-eyed, eager pilgrims immediately at ease by waving a warm hello with his huge restless, worker's hands, which now and then unconsciously finger the pectoral cross or adjust the papal skullcap. He opens each encounter with his favorite words: *"Sia lodato Gesu Cristo!"* (Praised be Jesus Christ!) and follows with a brief spiritual thought. The enormously popular Pontiff (even pop records have been produced about him) then, if time allows, passes from person to person exchanging pleasantries in an amazing array of languages. John Paul II speaks excellent English, French, Italian and German in addition to his native Polish. An eternal student, the Pope took a cram course in Spanish just prior to his visit to Mexico in 1979. At synods and other official ecclesiastical sessions he speaks a flawless Latin.

Everyone is struck by his evident sanctity, gentleness, dignity, warmth, magnetism and easy but glowing smile.

He loves to joke and make his visitors laugh and a good deal of his humor is self-deprecatory, yet in such good taste that it never impairs but rather elevates his papal dignity. (For example at a meeting with journalists when he was Cardinal Wojtyla, one reporter asked about his exceptional love for skiing. Wojtyla, who always held his fellow Polish cardinal, Stefan Wyszynski, in lofty esteem, replied: "In Poland 40% of the cardinals ski." Reminded that there were only two Polish cardinals, Wojtyla rejoined: "In Poland, Wyszynski counts for 60%.")

When he is finished granting these audiences, the Pope will consume what's left of the morning, and the early part of the afternoon, meeting with cardinals and other Curia officials on Church government business. Each diocesan bishop throughout the world must make a quinquennial *ad limina* (at the threshold) report to the Pope on the state of his diocese. This time may also be used for such conferences.

But if it is Wednesday, he will instead proceed from these small private audiences to the grand weekly public audience which used to be held in the Basilica but which is now conducted, in good weather, in the great square and otherwise in the new Hall of Audiences, which with its sloping theater-like floor and its stage affords an unobstructed view for everyone. An elevator takes John Paul and his aides down to the Courtyard of Sixtus II. There his chauffeur will be waiting with the Mercedes to drive his beloved Pontiff around the back of St. Peter's over to the hall, a ride of about two minutes, with exquisite views of the Vatican Gardens all along the way. The hall is filled to overflowing, close to ten thousand, and has been filling up from as early as eight o'clock. At a minute or two past eleven, the big curtains in the rear of the *Aula delle Udienze* are drawn and the Pope appears, almost magically, like a wonderful vision. As did his immediate predecessor, John Paul II has chosen to dispense with the Sedia Gestatoria, the portable throne on which the pontiff would be borne into the hall or into the great basilica, and instead walks slowly down the center aisle stopping to pat a face, or lift an infant (he's simply wild about kids), or cover his ears with his hands pretending to be deafened by the roar of emotion that always greets him. As hearty and enthusiastic applause and cries of *"Viva Il Papa!"* roll in waves from the back of the hall in the wake of his passing, John Paul's eyes dart left and right, his right hand making, over and over, the sign of the cross in all directions, his arms opening wide in a paternal, embracing gesture until he reaches the front of the auditorium and mounts the huge stage, backdropped by Raphael's magnificent tapestry of the Resurrection. Stern-faced Swiss Guards stand as colorful sentinels around the hall while plainclothes Vatican security agents nervously study the throng.

After the thunderous ovation subsides, the Pope begins, with his booming voice, his weekly talk, in Italian. This takes anywhere from twenty minutes to a half hour. Then John Paul II gives a capsule version of his sermon in French, German, Spanish, Portuguese, English and, of course, in his native Polish. Then he imparts his Apostolic Benediction, in Latin, and receives another tumultuous tribute from the people who would like to see the audience go on and on.

With the applause and *vivas* ringing in his ears, Pope John Paul descends the stairs and walks along the front row to speak to the people fortunate enough to have obtained seats there. Among them might be a foreign V.I.P., an old priest who views this as the highlight of his priesthood, a group of nuns from Calabria seeing the Vicar of Christ for the first time, a journalist from America, bike racers from Sardinia, a small group of chefs from France, some of John Paul's own children from the Diocese of Rome.

Sometimes it is arranged for a group to perform for him. Perhaps some Polish singers, or Venezuelan dancers, perhaps a troupe of jugglers from Belgium. For most people the Papal audience is the emotional climax of their trip to Rome. For the Pope is Rome. Seeing the Holy Father for the first or hundredth time is an indescribable thrill for everyone, regardless of religious persuasion. His appearance among the throng, or merely at his window high over St. Peter's Square, evokes a unanimous, genuine joy, a joy that reaches back through time to Peter himself, the first bearer of the "awful keys" as Oscar Wilde has called them. This continuity of emotion at the sight of the terrestrial Vicar of Christ led Chesterton to remark that, "The Church grows young while the world grows old."

(To participate in the Wednesday general audience one ought to apply a few days in advance to his or her nation's diplomatic representative to the Holy See. Americans may obtain passes from the Rector of the North American College in Rome, Via del'Umiltà, 30.)

We especially enjoy the audiences in July, August, and the first part of September when the Pope is in residence at the Papal summer retreat in the picturesque hill town of Castel Gandolfo. There each summer Wednesday and Sunday a festive atmosphere prevails. The public parking lots on the edge of town are jammed with tourist' buses and the sloping serpentine, medieval, cobblestoned streets are clogged with souvenir and religious article stands and with people from every land. The Papal Villa is perched on the summit of this Alban Hill overlooking placid Lake Albano. Thus, in the hours preceding the general audience, the river of humanity flows uphill through vineyards and olive groves. For an hour or so after the Pope's appearance, it cascades back toward the edge of town and the parking areas, and then, for the most part, back to Rome.

On Wednesday John Paul II gives the general audience in the vast new Audience Hall started in the reign of Pius XII and opened under John XXIII. Sunday at noon the Pope appears on his little balcony facing the large courtyard in the center of the villa, while the overflow crowd packs the village square out in front of the Papal residence. After his short talk to the thousands in the courtyard, the Pope walks over to the third floor balcony on the front side of the building to say a few words to and impart his blessing on the townspeople and their visitors in the lovely piazza. The villagers love their number one citizen and are much indebted to him for the shot of adrenalin his summer stay gives to the local economy.

We like to make a day of it out here. If I am working at my part time job as a guide and am conducting a group to the audience, some of my family will accompany me. If I have a free day we usually take a couple of neighborhood kids along with our own and come out early and stay late. Some of our friends in the Vatican guard are on summer assignment here and by visiting with them we get to stroll in the wonderful Papal Gardens. Midst such serene beauty, it is easy to see why five centuries of pontiffs have elected to spend the summer season here.

On the last Sunday of this past August we stood in the courtyard and heard a flock of nuns from Spain serenade the smiling Pontiff and when they were through, a crack, all-girls drum and bugle corps from Quebec put on a thrilling show for John Paul and the rest of us and, upon conclusion of the Pope's appearance, marched in formation through the huge gate of the villa on through the piazza, down the spaghetti-like streets back to their buses, accompanied all the way by the village kids running along the high narrow sidewalks.

As the Pope returned to his quarters for a light lunch we stopped in a local *alimentaria* and put together a brown-bag lunch of *prosciutto* and *formaggio* and then drove about a mile out to a little cafe with a terrace and tables high over the lake, where we feasted and discussed the exciting events of the day thus far.

Now let us shift the scene back to Rome. The general audience takes an hour and a half or more and so it is often past one in the afternoon when the Pope returns to his Vatican apartment for lunch, which for him is not the main meal of the day as it had been in previous pontificates, but a mere snack. The typical menu is some bread, and cheese, or some biscuits, washed down with light tea or buttermilk. Joining the Pope at lunch will be, more likely than not, some close aides and on occasion maybe a visiting bishop, or the Secretary of State, or an old friend from Wojtyla's years in Rome as a student at the Pontifical Angelicum University.

The tables of other Popes were also rather frugal. Pope Leo XIII, for example, took only black coffee for breakfast; a slice of meat, a vegetable, a piece of fruit and a glass of claret at midday; and at supper, which was sometimes as late as ten o'clock, an egg and a salad. Benedict XV ate not for pleasure but solely to fuel his frail body for more mileage in his work. Pius XI's supper consisted of two eggs, bread, and white wine. (Upon election to the Chair of Peter he had given up his favorite post-supper cigar. He thought it unfavorable for the Pontifical image.) Pius XII ate like a bird. Those close to him were convinced that when he did eat, it was just for diversion or as a grudging concession to one of life's exigencies. Pope St. Pius X and another heavyweight, Pope John XXIII, enjoyed eating but never overate.

John Paul naps for half hour or so after lunch and then begins the second part of his day as he did the first, in the chapel in prayer and meditation. This is followed by a period of relaxation. In the best tradition of many of his predecessors for hundreds of years, John Paul II likes to walk in the lush Vatican Gardens, though he dislikes the security commotion his daily walk in the gardens causes. Late in his reign Paul VI had a terrace built over the roof of his bedroom. When pressed for time, John Paul II will skip the gardens and use the terrace to "take the air" as the Romans say, among the many potted plants and under the lovely ivy-colored pergola, and to delight in one of the best vistas of his beloved adopted hometown, *Bella Roma.*

Each noon, Leo XIII could be found wandering in the sprawling *Giardini Vaticani*. In summer he would schedule his daily constitutional stroll for the evening when the heat had abated somewhat. As a nonagenarian he settled for a daily carriage ride around his miniature state. Pope Pius X used to be content to just sit in some shady nook of the gardens in early afternoon and unwind by reading or catnapping or listening to the fountains or watching the lizards play tag among the shrubs. Benedict XV, busy with the diplomatic problems of wartime, allowed himself no such recess. Pius XI would ride around the gardens a few times in an open-top car. Papa Pacelli, Pius XII, deeply loved to walk off his worries and tensions every day without fail, rain or shine, in the fragrant air of the gardens which are a harmonious blend of beauty, tranquillity, and solitude. Water provides the background music as it plays on bronze and marble statues in the fountains that seem to be ubiquitous in this sanctuary. Late in his life when his physicians worried about Pius walking in the driving rains of a *tramontana,* he had a solitary stretch of stone wall built from east to west. On the south side of this forty-foot high, yellowish, vine-covered wall, Pacelli could enjoy his promenade even on a rainy day, somewhat protected from the wetness and winds sweeping down from the Alps. John XXIII used his garden walks to get to know the Vatican workmen. But many times he was eager, like the current occupant of the Chair of Peter, to take his stroll out in the streets of Rome to mingle with his diocesan flock. So frequently did he exit from the Vatican, in fact, that one punster journalist called him, "John Outside the Walls," a take-off on the name of the patriarchal Basilica of St. Paul's Outside the Walls.

This daily garden interlude is only one of many common denominators of the lives of the most recent pontiffs. All were extraordinarily self-disciplined individuals with an equally extraordinary capacity for long, hard work hours. They set a demanding pace for themselves and expected the same from those around them. They set a high priority on punctuality, and all shared a disdain for indecision, wordiness, pettiness or any other enemy of the most precise, efficacious use of time. Benedict XV was so fanatically punctual he once allowed his barber to precede a cardinal who was a couple of minutes late. On the ride to Castel Gandolfo Pius XII, anxious to get to his desk, used to prod his chauffeur: *Presto! Presto!* (Faster! Faster!)

Each was gifted, as is John Paul II, with a rapid, incisive mind and the ability to listen to a complex report and go right to the essence of the matter. All got by on little sleep and shared a disregard, if not a contempt, for physical comfort. All were incurable scholars and spent their sparse free moments in either the sanctification of the soul or the cultivation of the intellect. All of them were fine linguists. John Paul II, too, is the embodiment of all these traits.

After the stroll on his terrace Pope John Paul returns to his private study adjacent to his bedroom and there spends the rest of the afternoon and early evening working on his weekly message or his brief Sunday sermon (which he delivers at noon from the window of his study to the multitude gathered in St. Peter's Square) or Papal encyclicals, bulls, motu proprios and other official documents. He may also use some of this time on personal correspondence, or in the consideration of prospects for the episcopate, or on budgetary matters. The only change in this schedule might be the Pope's attendance at some crisis meeting with Curia leaders. (Halfway through this rigorous private work session, Sister might bring in an *espresso.)*

The Pope's study, with its well-stocked bookcases, enormous antique desk, and white telephone (number 698-3131), fosters an ambience conducive to such intellectually demanding activity, although there is a television set and soft leather armchair that must create a slight temptation from time to time for the busy pontiff. (One Sunday at his window, he—only half-jokingly—told the crowd gathered in the square for his noontime message and blessing that he had to cut short his remarks because an important televised soccer match, which he had waited all week to watch, was about to come on the air.)

Time evaporates all too quickly for the busy Supreme Pastor. All afternoon long the big bells of St. Peter's and those of the Court of St. Damasus boom out and tick off the hours and the quarter hours but go largely unnoticed by the engrossed Pontiff. But in the late afternoon his boundless nervous energy usually causes the Holy Father to heave his huge white-robed frame out of his chair and to move about this "little country of the soul," often dropping in on the people in their respective offices or workshops, sharing with them a cup of espresso while discussing the work they're doing, or inquiring about their families, or just making small talk about their weekend plans, their coming vacations, etc.

Around six in the evening the Pope will usually meet with Vatican protocol officials regarding the next day's audience schedule.

Darkness—in summer the apricot glow of the *tramonto*—reminds Il Papa that it is indeed late and way past time to eat. Before dinner, however, there might be another brief interlude on the terrace to enjoy watching the lights twinkle on in the villages of the distant Castelli. Dinner is normally served about eight. Not a fussy eater, John Paul II enjoys and finishes anything put in front of him, generously complimenting the cooking after each course. But he is obviously extra delighted when on occasion they surprise him with genuine Polish fare (particularly *pierogis* and *Kielbasa*). A non-smoker and a light drinker, the Holy Father will concede himself one glass of wine, usually white. Over dinner there are often last minute discussions of important matters. When the dishes are cleared the television set is turned on so that His Holiness can catch the evening newscast.

From here it's often back out on the rooftop terrace for John Paul, alone, to walk and read the breviary, or to formulate plans for his next journey. Before it gets too late he will step back inside and gather his household for a recitation of the Rosary.

By ten-thirty everyone else has departed and His Holiness returns to his lonely study for another three hours of work at his desk. The Vatican is in darkness now except for the illuminated fountains in the square, the soft floodlights that play on the cupola, and the patch of yellow light in the second window from the right on the top floor of the Apostolic Palace. Yet, for the Pope, the long, long day is still not over.

(Changes in this daily routine are occasioned only by special receptions, beatification and canonization ceremonies, consistories, and the like. One day a year the Pope attends, in the Sistine Chapel, a funeral Mass in memory of his predecessor. On another day he attends, in the same chapel, a Mass in honor of his elevation to the Pontificate.

Holy Week also brings great changes in the Pope's schedule. On Holy Thursday he pays visits to the major basilicas of Rome. On Good Friday he returns to San Giovanni in Laterano where he symbolically washes the feet of twelve seminarians. Late that evening he proceeds by motorcade to the Colosseum and walks the last few hundred yards of the route bearing a huge wooden cross into the arena where so many early disciples of Christ were martyred on orders of the Imperial government.

On the feast of the Immaculate Conception, December 8, the Holy Father rides in a carriage to Piazza di Spagna where he lays a wreath at the monumental column crowned by a statue of Mary Conceived Without Sin. On Sunday afternoons, taking his primary title of Bishop of Rome very seriously, he goes out into the city, visiting a different parish each week.)

During the final quiet hours, at his old wooden desk, John Paul II must, on some evenings, grow acutely aware of the profound loneliness of his job. But, for him, the day will be done only when he has extracted every last ounce of energy in his mind and limbs. At that point, he lays down his pen, rubs his tired eyes, rises and stretches. To wind down the machinery of his brilliant mind he sits back in a soft chair and listens for a quarter hour while Chopin or Corelli or Vivaldi or Bach or perhaps Mozart performs, on the stereo set.

Then the Vicar of Christ on Earth drops to his knees to offer his night prayers, a simple ritual he has performed every night of his life since he was a frail five-year-old lad in the sleepy Polish village of Wadowice, 170 miles south of Warsaw. His series of Our Fathers and Hail Marys completed, John Paul II makes a fervent Act of Contrition.

He meditates a few moments longer, gets up, switches off the light. Vatican City is completely still. The Pope too must sleep.

7

"Go and Preach Ye All Nations"

From early on in his reign John Paul II has embraced, with unexampled vigor, Christ's mandate to the first bishops of the Church, the Apostles. From the dusty streets of a backwater Mexican village, to the country roads of the American heartland, to the tree-lined boulevards of the French capital, this Holy Father has already in his young reign traveled farther and more frequently than any other previous Roman pontiff. And he has replayed the following dramatic scene wherever he has gone: When the gleaming jet bearing Christ's Vicar pulls to a complete stop, the throng gathered at the edge of the tarmac grows momentarily still, while a rolling staircase is put into place. Then a by-now familiar ritual begins, midst tumultuous applause. An imposing figure in white and red appears smiling at the door of the aircraft, returns the waves of his ecstatic spiritual children, slowly descends, and after the last step drops to his hands and knees and kisses the ground as a gesture of love to his host country. Pope John Paul has come to still another nation to preach the Good News, to comfort, to encourage, to inspire his fellow Christians in these often frightening times of ours.

These "pilgrimages of faith," as His Holiness likes to call his trips abroad, began with a journey to Mexico in late January of 1979, with a visit, en route, to the Dominican Republic.

For six days the indefatigable Pope crisscrossed Mexico, giving dozens of speeches, riding in daily motorcades atop a white fire truck specially tailored for the occasion so that the millions along the papal route could get a good, though fleeting, look at the successor of St. Peter. Wherever he traveled the Holy Father was greeted with a spectacular outpouring of love from his flock. Church bells pealed joyously while confetti, balloons, doves, and even fireworks filled the skies. Catholics, indeed people of all faiths, who just a short time ago would never have even dreamed of seeing a Pope, cheered thunderously as John Paul II passed their vantage points. For all of them, the young and the old, the affluent and the poor, the devout and the indifferent alike, it was a never-to-be-forgotten experience. And at the end of the 15,000 mile itinerary John Paul II appeared remarkably as vibrant as he had in Santo Domingo.

Five months later, in balmy June weather, John Paul left the Vatican once again on a heart-rending glorious visit to his beloved homeland of Poland. A Pope behind the Iron Curtain!

From the moment his Alitalia 727 deposited him in the airport at Warsaw, the Pope was happily mobbed by his laughing, weeping, admiring countrymen. Grammar school children in their academic frocks, teenagers wearing T shirts with Karol Wojtyla's image, pretty girls in native costume, helmeted coalminers, and babushkaed grandmothers roared their welcome to 'little Lolek' as he was called in boyhood. Everywhere were the colors of the Pope's two nations—the yellow and white of the Vatican side by side with the red and white of Poland.

And there was no mistaking the emotional impact of all this on the Pontiff. At times his face would break into that great smile. At other times his eyes would brim with tears from a severe attack of beautiful nostalgia. Often he would break from the formal procession and rush into the crowd to oblige the people who so dearly wanted to touch him, to look into his eyes, to be patted on the cheek by his tender, paternal hands. He would toss children into the air, sending them into gales of laughter. He would hug their elders and throw a bear-hug around old acquaintances in the Polish hierarchy. From Warsaw to Czestochowa, to his hometown of Wadowice, Pope John II thrilled his countrymen by his personal magnetism and awed them with his obvious sanctity. He celebrated outdoor Masses for hundreds of thousands at a time. After many of them he would join the throng in a Polish song-fest, his rich baritone voice booming out over the P.A. system. At one stop, Gniezno, with the adorable innocence of a little boy, he asked after one song: "What shall we sing next?"

At the airport for his departure the multitude wept, and the Holy Father's eyes brimmed with tears again as everyone realized that he would most likely never again see his dear homeland.

In the autumn of 1979 the pilgrim pope was off to Ireland en route to America. Everywhere that John Paul went during his three days on the Emerald Isle he saw enthusiastic crowds stretching to the horizon, at Dublin, at Limerick, at Knock—and pleaded with them again and again to put an end to the religious violence that has wracked their beautiful land.

On a rainy first of October the Pontiff arrived at Boston's Logan International Airport to start an unforgettable tour of several principal American cities—Boston, New York, Chicago, Philadelphia, and Washington—and the rolling farmlands of the midwest, creating a joyful hysteria wherever he went, offering an outdoor Mass at each stop. At the United Nations in New York he spoke with a fiery eloquence for world peace. In Washington he was received at the White House by President Carter.

On the evening of October 2, I had the good fortune of covering the Papal Mass at Yankee Stadium for a leading Catholic magazine, *Our Sunday Visitor,* and for a number of secular newspapers. The following account is drawn from my journalist's diary. Might I share with you one of the most treasured experiences of my life, describing as candidly and as vividly as I can, what it felt like to be present at the Holy Father's liturgy that evening:

Yankee Stadium
New York—October 2, A.D. 1979
5:25 P.M.

One autumn day, almost two thousand years ago, the Supreme Pontiff of the Catholic Church made a personal appearance in a huge stadium with an overflow crowd in the world's principal city of the time. That gentle, husky, rugged, white-haired first Bishop of Rome, who had come from a distant land, was escorted into the noisy arena by a small group of soldiers who would shortly assist at his crucifixion at mid-field. His attire consisted of tatters, manacles, and fetters.

On this autumn evening, a little more than two hours from now, the Supreme Pontiff of the Catholic Church will make a personal appearance in a huge stadium with an overflow crowd in the world's principal city of our time. This gentle, husky, rugged, white-haired 265th Bishop of Rome who has come from a distant land will be escorted into the noisy arena by a small group of his fellow bishops who will shortly assist at his Pontifical Mass near second base. His attire will consist of a miter, a chasuble, and a staff crowned with a crucifix.

This evening the eighty thousand of us gathered here will witness a dramatic and solemn testimonial to the Church's triumph over its ancient and modern oppressors.

My wife and I made the drive in from Jersey earlier this afternoon and arrived just before the gates of the Ballpark-become-Church were opened at five p.m. The first thing that caught our attention when we entered

was the neon-lit playback screen in centerfield display-
ing Pope John Paul II's coat of arms. Our eyes then soon
focused on the splendor of the Papal Altar, the platform
for which stretches from second base out into short centerfield, right where Di Maggio was wont to make his
effortless shoestring catches.

The deck and the steps leading to it are carpeted in
regal red. On either side of the white altar, which faces
home plate, stand three tall bronze candelabra whose
candles have already been lit in anticipation of the
solemn Mass that is scheduled to begin at eight. To the
extreme right of the platform there is a bronze ten-foot
high crucifix, and to the extreme left a white lectern. At
the foot of the steps we notice two icons—one of Jesus,
the other of his Virgin Mother—representing the Eastern rites of the Church. From the base of the staircase to
a point several yards back of homeplate stretches a ten
foot wide red runner which, in dissecting the green
of the infield, gives the playing area the look of
an enormous gift-wrapped Christmas package. (Which
strikes me as altogether fitting, for I consider Karol
Wojtyla as the Holy Spirit's special gift to our era.)

Over the altar is a canopy, supported by four thin
poles, fringed in yellow and white, the colors of the
Vatican State Flag. Flower beds of yellow and white
chrysanthemums moat the stage.

High atop the facade of the bleacher section flap
twenty-two flags, eleven of our Stars and Stripes alter-
nating with eleven banners of the Pope's tiny country.
Yellow and white bunting graces the railings of all three
tiers all around the stadium. Even the two foul poles
continue this color scheme.

6:00 P.M.

Vendors have begun their appointed rounds
throughout the "church" hawking medals, posters, pen-
nants, programs, all with John Paul's image. One also
hears the plaintive and familiar cry of "Hot Dogs! Soda!
Peanuts!" ("This, I muse to myself, is carrying the

reforms of the Second Vatican Council just a bit too far." Well at least beer is conspicuous by its absence.)

But many in the crowd, I notice, have decided to fight the good fight against inflation by bringing their own fixin's from home in picnic baskets and shopping bags.

Missallettes are now being distributed, free of charge. Their covers bear a line drawing of the Holy Father and this verse from the Eighty-Fifth Psalm:

"Justice Shall March Before Him, And Peace Shall Follow His Steps."

6:15

The arc lights have just been turned on to illuminate the spectacle taking shape. Finished with today's New York Times and even with its crossword puzzle, Camille and I turn to reading the dozens of banners on display. "I love you, Holy Father," proclaims one in the third deck of right field. "Viva Il Papa!" declares another. Behind the Yankee dugout there's a one word sign: "Stolat!" (Polish for: "May He live a hundred years!") But my favorite is the adorable one that reads: "Oh My Papa." A charcoal fresco on heavy brown paper, masking-taped to the mezzanine near third base, bears this wish: "Long Live Pope John Paul II."

Back down here on the playing field thousands of wooden chairs have been set up to accommodate the press, dignitaries, members of the hierarchy, the clergy and religious orders and specially invited guests. In the chairs to the left rear of the altar sit the musicians and the choir. Hundreds of priests in black cassocks and white surplices, Franciscan friars in their coffee-brown robes, nuns in habits of assorted shades, monsignori in their black soutanes with purple sashes and purple buttons and piping, bishops in their crimson, Knights of Columbus—serving as ushers—in their yellow capes and yellow plumed hats, render the area around the altar a festival of colors. The people up in the stands, for the most part, owe their presence here tonight to their luck in the parish lottery. Twenty tickets were allocated to each parish in the metropolitan area, and most pastors decided to use the lottery system for their dissemination. Not too far from where we are sitting is a Polish American group in the native dress of their ancestral homeland in honor of Papa Wojtyla.

6:40

This is my first visit to the "House that Ruth Built" since its facelifting a few years ago. I notice that the monuments—to the Babe, Gehrig, and other pin-striped immortals—which were once part of the playing field are now in a cyclone fence enclosure behind the center-field wall. Out in the Yankee bullpen in right field the specially renovated Ford Bronco—quickly nicknamed the "Popemobile"—is poised for its brief but historic spin around the arena. The visitor's bullpen has an ambulance ready for any unfortunate emergency.

The murmur of the crowd rises a few decibels as the two dugouts suddenly fill to the brim with cops. This we are told is the greatest security arrangement in our nation's history. Vatican gendarmes will be, throughout the Pope's stay in the United States this week, comrades-in-arms of the Secret Service. And they will be backed up tonight by fifteen hundred New York City policemen, a veritable army in navy blue.

The evening is overcast, with a mild breeze. Some members of the Supreme Pastor's flock were providential enough to come prepared with afghans and heavy sweaters for the inevitable sharp drop in temperature before the evening's end. Curiosity getting the better of him, that old devil moon can't help peeking down at the grand and colorful pageant every now and then.

As the huge clock in the outfield wall prepares to mark seven, the choir and the musicians take their "batting practice," rehearsing some of the hymns for tonight's Mass.

7:23

Another murmur ripples through the throng and I look up from my notes to see why. Billy Martin, the

Yankee Skipper, in blue blazer, red shirt open at the neck, has just come to the top step of the dugout to survey things. But there'll be no umpires for him to do battle with in tonight's event. The stadium is now about ninety-five percent full. Mayor Koch arrives to warm applause. Politics are suspended for tonight. Tonight all of us here belong to the same party, the Party of Humankind, the Party of Brotherhood, the Party of Love so eloquently advocated by the Pilgrim of Peace who has come all the way from the banks of the Tiber to the banks of the Hudson to lead us in prayer for a better world.

7:42

Governor Carey and Senator Moynihan cause a stir with their arrival and take their seats alongside the Mayor in the section to the left front of the altar.

8:01

The Pope is late! But everyone understands, for his has been a most incredibly busy day. Over in nearby Cardinal Hayes High School he is at last getting a chance for a bite to eat, after which he will make his way through the tragic streets of Harlem and the South Bronx, giving hope and joy to the people there via the special magic of his inspirational words and smile and innerglow.

8:45

Evidently word has been received that the Pontiff's arrival is imminent for there is a stir in the security forces, the head lights of the Popemobile have been turned on, and a group of prelates in their white miters (the pointed hats that represent episcopal authority) have gathered at home plate. The vendors have all vanished.

Now, just five minutes later, the blare of trumpets resounds throughout the cavernous amphitheater and the Holy Father comes into view out in the bullpen, boards the little white truck with the Papal symbol painted on its roof, and is borne through the bullpen gates and onto the warning track as the multitude erupts in a joyous and deafening ovation as a million flashbulbs wink like oversized fireflies at the unbelievable scene. As the vehicle swings right and at five m.p.h. makes its way around the field, its smiling passenger waves paternally to his deliriously happy spiritual children. Riding with His Holiness is the Archbishop of New York, Terence Cardinal Cooke.

At homeplate John Paul disembarks and follows his brothers in the Episcopate in solemn procession to the platform. He climbs the stairs, bows to kiss the altar and exclaims to the excited throng: "Praised be Jesus Christ!" The Mass has begun.

(At the Pontiff's elbow constantly throughout the Mass will be the professional-looking Monsignor Virgilio Noè, the Master of Ceremonies at all Papal rituals and the second most photographed person in the Catholic Church. Sometimes referred to as the Holy Father's shadow, Monsignor Noè is a familiar sight in the little streets of the Vatican. On summer mornings when my work brings me into Vatican City I often cross paths with the monsignor and always get a courtly "Buon Giorno" from him. Walking briskly, the slim figure in black cassock with attache case in right hand draws awed glances from everyone and a salute from the medieval-clad Swiss Guards.)

This is the second Pontifical Mass in the history of this famed baseball park. Nearly fourteen years ago to the day, to the hour, (October 4, 1965) Pope Paul VI celebrated the Sacred Mysteries at the very same spot.

The Mass will be in two traditional parts: The Liturgy of the Word, centering on the reading of Scripture, and the Liturgy of the Eucharist whose focal point will be the consecration of the bread and wine.

To demonstrate vividly the universality of the Church, this evening's Mass will use ten languages: English, Spanish, Italian, Polish, German, French, Chinese, Ukrainian, Gaelic, and Latin.

We have come now to the first reading. Helen Hayes, the renowned American actress, is approaching the lectern where she will read from the Book of Genesis. For the much-esteemed Miss Hayes, clad in white long-sleeved blouse and ankle-length green skirt, this will be the most important and most thrilling role of her long career—and surely the largest audience.

9:30

The Holy Father is about to deliver his homily. He will remain seated throughout to signify his teaching authority. While a small plane with wing lights twinkling floats its way overhead to La Guardia the Pope begins his message. It is a simple yet profound one warning against the perils of materialism and hedonism and calling for a return to the simpler and purer life.

"The poor of the United States and of the world are your brothers and sisters in Christ," the Pope reminds us. "You must never be content to leave them just the crumbs from the feast. And you must treat them like guests at your table." He also draws our attention to the parable of the rich man and Lazarus, a beggar who was rewarded in the next life while the rich man was damned for his lack of concern for a fellowman: "We cannot stand idly by when thousands of humans are dying of hunger. We cannot stand idly by enjoying our own riches and freedom if in any place the Lazarus of the twentieth century stands at our door."

Following the climactic point of the Mass—the Consecration—hundreds of priests fan out and up through the stadium to distribute the Eucharist while the multitude joins the choir in singing the Lord's Prayer. (There is a certain sense of unreality about everything unfolding before me tonight, and I am hard put to convince myself that I am not dreaming. At this moment I feel like I have suddenly been transported back through time and space to the Miracle of the Loaves and Fishes.)

It is nearly eleven o'clock now as His Holiness concludes the Holy Sacrifice. We begin to sing the old hymn, "Holy God, We Praise Thy Name..." while Pope

John Paul II removes his Mass vestments and over his white soutane, with its cape mischievously flapping in the wind, puts on the full-length red cloak called a "mantello" and the small white skull cap or "zucchetto." John Paul has now come to the front of the platform as the breeze tosses his wispy hair all over his forehead. This along with his innocent smile, his rosy cheeks, his glistening eyes, and his handsome Slavic features give him the angelic look of a little boy, of "Lolec" as his family and friends used to affectionately call him in his youth back in the sleepy village of Wadowice. Again the ovation begins, cascading in an ear-splitting roar down from the upper reaches of the third tier through the mezzanine and lower level. Down on the field wave upon wave of applause crests at the beginning of the platform and then crashes joyfully at the feet of the beaming Pontiff.

All about me people of both genders, of all ages, all classes, all colors, and perhaps—just perhaps—of all creeds are weeping from sheer joy yet through their tears they are smiling and despite the lumps in their throats are managing to chant rhythmically and louder and louder in a delirious outpouring of filial love: "Long live the Pope! Long live the Pope! Long live the Pope!!!" A woman reporter from the Polish American press implores me to tell her that this is truly happening, that it is not merely a wonderful dream. I lift her six-year-old son to my shoulders to improve his vantage point on this never-to-be-forgotten vignette of history. I can imagine him eighty years from now bouncing his great grandson on his knee and telling him about that long ago night in Yankee Stadium. The night is nearly over now as His Holiness descends the steps and walks slowly along the carpet toward home plate. En route he too picks up a little boy who has slipped through the cordon of guards, holds the lucky lad aloft to the delight of everyone.

So that we his spiritual children might get still one more chance to look lovingly into his eyes, Pope John Paul II, weary but warmed by our response to him, boards the Tonka-like truck for another spin around the warning track. Then suddenly, oh so suddenly and so peacefully, like a true apparition, he fades from view.

———————

Since his triumphant visit to the United States Pope John Paul has added France and Japan to his travel record and in late November of 1980 hurriedly left the Vatican once again, this time to visit and comfort the victims of the awful earthquakes in southern Italy.

8

Vaticanus Subterraneus

To grasp fully the significance of the Vatican in modern times one must have a knowledge of the early centuries of Christianity, when the Church in a fierce struggle for survival, literally went underground. Long ages before the Christians of Rome were able to worship their God in the unexampled splendor of the churches and basilicas one sees throughout the Eternal City today, our spiritual forebears were practicing their faith and celebrating the Holy Sacrifice of the Mass, at great peril to themselves, in tunnels they had originally dug as burial grounds. To understand the Church of Rome today one must first understand the catacombs of Peter's day. To appreciate the architectural splendor and prestige and significance of the Church headquarters on Vatican Hill today, one must first comprehend the bleakness and human misery of the Church quartered in the subsoil of the Roman countryside in Imperial times.

Let us address ourselves now to that sad yet glorious chapter in the history of the institutional Church, the period of the Catacombs. Let us discuss the ancient underground cemeteries which by virtue of the Lateran treaty are considered extraterritorial Vatican.

One of the most intellectually and ethnically fashionable words of our time is the term "roots." The fabulously successful novel by Alex Haley—and the widely-acclaimed television version of it—has in recent years set untold thousands off on a feverish quest for more information about their pasts.

Precisely four centuries ago—in late 1578 and early 1579—something occurred just outside the ancient red-brick walls of Rome that precipitated a wave of excitement in the Eternal City and which ultimately paved the way for Christians of subsequent centuries to examine and renew, in the most vivid manner conceivable, their spiritual "roots." It was at that time that workmen digging in the fields of the lovely and serene Roman countryside were daily coming upon entrance shafts —for long centuries concealed from view—to the subterranean cemeteries of the earliest Christians. Out along the Via Salaria, the old salt road, for instance, a group of laborers digging, under a golden Mediterranean sky, for pozzuolana, a volcanic material ideal for making cement, found a marvelously preserved burial ground with countless corridors on numerous levels.

By the score, clerical scholars, bishops, cardinals, and even Pope Gregory XIII himself, descended into the dank and eerie tunnels to study by candlelight the epitaphs and frescoes and religious objects left there by our spiritual forebears almost a score of centuries ago.

Haphazard techniques of exploring and digging out the galleries, unused for a millenium and filled up by the shifting sands of time, gave way gradually to the marvelous methods of modern archeology. One of the pioneers of the organized excavating of these sacred places, Antonio Bosio, became known even in his lifetime as "the Columbus of the Catacombs." For the most up-to-date techniques—and discoveries—in this field, however, we are indebted to Giovanni Battista De Rossi of the mid-19th century.

In fact, to all the people involved back then —workmen, scholars, patrons of sacred archeology, as well as to the archeologists themselves—we disciples of Christ today owe an enormous debt. It is due to their tireless collective efforts to uncover our Church's past that we can, in our time, make a pilgrimage to the seat of Christendom and go down deep into its very earth to pray at the tombs of the martyrs, to read their tender professions of faith in the Lord, to take inspiration from the many artistic expressions of their love for Him.

And speaking of debt, the early Christians of Rome owed one themselves—regarding the idea of underground cemeteries—to the Jewish community of the imperial capital. Through writings still extant of both pagan and Christian literati, we learn that there was such a community on the banks of the Tiber long anterior to the Christian era. In the late first century B.C., the Roman Jews discovered that the volcanic, chocolate-fudge-like subsoil of the region readily lent itself to tunneling while at the same time remaining supportive of the ground above. Jewish catacombs were soon after established, just beyond the shadows of the city's soaring fortifications, along such venerable highways as the Via Nomentana, the Via Labicana, and the great south road, the Via Appia. Since many of the earliest Christians in the city came from the Jewish populace it is only logical to infer that they continued the burial practices familiar to them.

In old Rome there was a law against interment within the city walls. Therefore all cemeteries—Pagan, Jewish, and Christian alike—had to be extramural. (Two emperors, Augustus and Hadrian, granted themselves dispensations from this statute and the ruins of their imposing mausolea are among the city's most illustrious land marks even to this day.) Cicero, in his dissertation *De Legibus,* alludes to the law: *"Hominem mortuum, inquit lex, in urbe ne sepelito."* (The law states that a deceased person may not be entombed inside the city.) And so too does a first-century writer thus: *"Intra muros civitatis corpus sepulturae dari non potest."* (Within the walls of the city a body may not be given to the grave.)

Out on the highways stretching in all directions to link the provinces with *Caput Mundi* (as the Romans proudly called their home town), the wealthy patrician classes bought tracts of land on which to build their stately mausolea, of brick understructures but veneered with marble and ornamented with statuary.

Since the Jews were out of the economic as well as the social mainstream of the capital, they could not afford to raise such grand funeral monuments. Necessity, then, mothered their invention of subterranean burial grounds which would be instituted in the following manner. First a shaft would be bored on an angle into the earth. That shaft, of sufficient width to allow the passage of an adult male, would then be stepped with brick and mortar. At the foot of the staircase a corridor about eight feet high and a couple of yards wide would be projected as far as the deed to the land above permitted. In the walls of the corridor, niches would be carved out with the dimensions of each contingent upon the size of the body to be entombed. The bereaved family would wrap the remains in linen and then place it in the small vault which would be closed with brick or tiles or a slab of marble whose edges would then be sealed with mortar. For the sake of future identification an epitaph would be scratched into the brick or engraved in the marble or in some cases painted on. From these messages, most of which are in Greek, for the Jews of Rome used that as their language, we learn that the Jewish Community enjoyed a certain freedom of worship, at least up until the reign of the demonic Caligula who made life wretched for Jews throughout the empire. One reads: "Here lies Annianus, son of Julianus, Father of the Synagogue of the Campesians (i.e., down in the Campus Martius quarter). Another translates to: "Here lies Pancharios, Father of the Synagogue of Elaea." And still more individual houses of Jewish worship are mentioned in the underground scrawlings.

Now when the original corridor was filled to its burial capacity, new galleries would be dug at right angles to it and in time corridors at right angles to the secondary galleries and parallel to the initial one would be excavated. Simple and orderly at first, this network of passages would usually grow more labyrinthine with time. After using every foot of space allowed by the property deed, the Jews and later also the Christians, would break through the floor of the original corridor, dig another angled shaft and start the process all over again, until, by the fourth century of our era some of the cemeteries consisted of five and even six levels of corridors with their niches.

In the second year of the reign of Claudius, some scholars believe, which could put it at the year 42, Peter, Prince of the Apostles and our first Pope, established his Holy See (i.e., diocese) in the city on the Tiber. Not long after, Paul, formerly a persecutor, now a propagator of the faith, entered Rome. The two Apostles quickly assumed the leadership of the small Christian community there.

During the next two decades our spiritual forebears were left unharassed by the authorities, practiced their faith openly, buried their dead in tunnels under the sun-baked Roman campagna.

Suddenly catastrophe!!! On July 19 of the year 64 a fire broke out that was to rage for more than a week and leave Rome a city of ashes. When the deranged Emperor Nero, seeking to exculpate himself from suspicions of arson, put the blame on the followers of Christ he set off three hundred years of Christian bloodbaths. These pogroms, which were carried out sporadically and with varying degrees of intensity, history calls "the persecutions." From this point on, the practice of the Christian religion became a serious crime, punishable by execution.

Now the Christians, who like the Jews had been all along in their brief history purchasing land outside the city for interment purposes and upon securing title duly recording said purchases with the official city register, were no longer free to worship as they chose. Whereas heretofore they would convene joyfully in one another's homes or in the residences of their bishops and priests to celebrate the sacred mysteries, they now had to be wary of police raids on such assemblies.

At this point they took to gathering midst their dead, down in their humble resting places which stood in stark contrast to the matchless splendor of the patrician tombs on the ground above. Down here for the next three centuries the courageous flock of Peter and his early successors could renew the Holy Sacrifice of Calvary, protected from the state by the state. A law against *violatio sepulcri,* which declared that all burial grounds were inviolable, was rigidly enforced. However even this law from time to time would be subverted by the same authorities sworn to uphold it. We have horrifying eyewitness accounts of Valerian's and other emperors' storm troopers smashing their way into the Christian cemeteries, killing priests and bishops (and occasionally even the Supreme Pontiffs) and then hauling off the faithful to the bar of Roman "justice."

Still, Tertullian writes, the more Rome tried to drown Christianity in her own blood, the more the blood of the martyrs became the seed of life for the new religion. *("Semen est sanguis Christianorum.")* Indeed the Christian community in Rome grew in great numbers, first among the Jews of the city and then among the poorer Pagan classes and finally among the Patrician and even Senatorial classes. By the late first century it had even reached into the Imperial family. We have documentary proof that Domitilla, cousin of the Christian-hating Emperor Domitian, embraced the faith and even gave over her private property for use as a Christian cemetery. This ground we know today as the Catacombs of Santa Domitilla.

By the early part of the fourth century there existed perhaps as many as seventy Christian cemeteries. Like many of ours today, these cemeteries were often named for a saint. Thus we hear of the cemetery of St. Sebastian, which because of its location in a natural depression along the Appian Way, became known specifically as *Sanctus Sebastianus Ad Catacumbas* (St. Sebastian in the Sunken Valley). In the Middle Ages the term "catacomb" came to be applied to all such burial places.

Then there are the Catacombs of St. Callistus, also on the Via Appia, of St. Agnes on the Via Nomentana, of St. Lawrence on the Via Tiburtina, of St. Pancratius on the Via Aurelia.

A tradition persists, backed by some archeological evidence, that during the particularly savage persecutions of Valerian in 258, the remains of Peter and Paul were removed from their respective tombs on the Vatican Hill and the Ostian Road (and subsequently transferred back). The Christians had grown increasingly worried that since these two graves were well known the government might have seen fit to destroy the relics of the Apostles.

The Christian catacombs were also distinguished by their graffiti, or epitaphs, which clearly proclaimed belief in the promise of the Resurrection. Prayers and Christian symbols such as the Fish, the anchor, the Keys of Peter abound in the "sunken valleys."

There were five burial arrangements down in the Christian catacombs with the niche in the wall (loculus) the most common. Another was the arcosolium, a recess in the wall with a capacity for four, five or six entombments. A Christian of some means might choose a sarcophagus, an ornate and usually sculptured casket of marble. Some people arranged for a cubiculum (small room) to be dug and to serve as a family sepulcher. These would often be veneered with stucco and the stucco frescoed with representations of Christ the Good Shepherd, the Last Supper, or some other Christian scene. The fifth and most humble type of burial was the forma, a sort of Potter's Field. This was merely a shallow trench in the floor of a corridor to receive the remains of a pauper.

Into the fresh mortar of the loculi and arcosoli would often be pressed coins for dating and identifying burial places. Another beautiful custom—and probably the forerunner of our practice of placing fresh flowers on a grave was that of embedding a small glass or vial filled with perfume into the mortar. Visitors to the crypt could then dip their fingers into these containers and in reverent memory of the departed loved one sprinkle his tomb with a few drops of the fragrance.

Illumination of these chilly passageways was achieved by occasional light shafts with grates in them flush with the ground overhead to prevent someone from falling in and also by small oil lamps called, in Latin, *luminaria.*

While there were, originally, numerous private burial societies that oversaw the digging and maintenance of the cemeteries, by the third century most of the catacombs had come under the direct administration of the Church.

With Constantine's edict from the northern city of Milan in 313 freeing the Christians to practice their faith and celebrate their rites openly and without fear, the catacombs had outlived their original purposes. But in the early Middle Ages, they were to take on a new usefulness, that as focal points of pilgrimages by Christians from all over the continent of Europe. Back then a paramount spiritual goal for a Christian was to go to Rome at least once in his or her lifetime, there to visit the greatest shrines of Christendom and also to descend *"ad catacumbas"* to pray at the tombs of those who died that the Church might live.

When Rome was ravaged by wave after wave of barbaric invaders in the fifth and sixth centuries the catacombs fell into total abandonment and remained in sepulchral stillness for a thousand years until the laborers on the Via Salaria initiated their rediscovery.

All Christians today whose personal economics allow for it ought to renew their faith and mark the second millennium of Mother Church by returning to their "roots" deep in the earth of the picturesque meadows surrounding the Eternal City.

...And so we came to Rome....

9

A Vatican Notebook

This city within a city, this state within a state is endlessly interesting and it is the aim of this chapter to itemize, and explain, some of the more interesting aspects of it. Should you some day have the opportunity to venture into this postage stamp-sized country, this chapter might serve you well as a sort of *vade mecum*.

THE VATICAN DISTRICT
IN THE DAYS OF PETER

In antiquity the whole area that sprawls between the Janiculum Hill and the Ponte Milvio, the bridge which carries the consular road, Via Flaminia, over the Tiber, was known as the Vatican. While there are several schools of thought on just what the word *"Vatican"* meant in old Latin, the prevailing opinion among today's classical scholars is that it derives from *Vaticinia,* meaning the oracles that were pronounced by the priests in charge of a local temple to Apollo, god of the arts. There were, incidentally, in classical times, other temples in this area, namely those in honor of Mars, Cybele, and Faunus.

Even the earliest Romans made a clear distinction with respect to the topography of the area, referring to *Montes Vaticani* (the Vatican Hills) and the *Ager Vaticanus* (the Vatican Plain). The plains were malarial and sparsely inhabited but the hills had a healthy air and hosted numerous dwellings. In time these slopes were quarried for earth to be used on various building projects by the Romans. This activity in time resulted in the deep valleys that we can clearly see today separating the Vatican from the Janiculum on one side and from Monte Mario on another.

In the late Republic the swampy Ager Vaticanus was drained and soon after prominent Romans established luxurious villas there. Olive groves, vineyards, statuary, fountains, arboreta proliferated and the area became one of the most fashionable districts of old Rome. The early empire witnessed a continued enthusiasm for the Vatican district. Caligula built a chariot track on the western slope of Vatican Hill and one of his successors, the equally deranged Nero, loved to race his chariot there to the carefully orchestrated ovation of the Romans that filled the arena to overflowing. (Tacitus writes: "Nero's passion was to race chariots in the Vatican Circus.")

Nero took such interest in the area that he laid out lavish gardens, the *Prata Neronis,* adjacent to the chariot track.

Ancient writings also reveal to us that two important roads, the Via Cornelia and the Via Triomphalis, passed through the Vatican quarter and linked it with the rest of the city.

PIAZZA SAN PIETRO

The great cobblestoned square of St. Peter, an ellipse 148 meters wide and 198 meters long, all enclosed by the colossal, statue-crowned, curved colonnade of Bernini, can be said to be the Vatican's lobby. For it is here that most first-time visitors enter the "Country of the Spirit." The colonnade, in whose cool forest of 284 columns I often take refuge from the sultry Roman summer, symbolizes the eternal loving embrace of Holy Mother Church for her children from all over the globe. Piazza San Pietro is further adorned by an exquisite center piece, an obelisk, 26 meters high, brought to Rome from Egypt by Caligula for the purpose of gracing the dividing island of his chariot course. This same soaring needle of granite looked down stoically while Peter, the first Bishop of Rome, suffered martyrdom before a screaming pagan mob. Now it is crowned with a bronze cross, that is actually a reliquary for it contains a piece of the True Cross, proclaiming the triumph of Christianity.

Flanking the obelisk and lending a marvelous symmetry to the "lobby" are twin baroque fountains, one by Stefano Maderno who executed the facade of the Basilica, framing the great dome with their slender silvery jets of water from the Vatican's aqueduct, the *Acqua Pia*.

This vast square has been the perennial setting for Papal drama. Here the faithful have witnessed events both joyous and sad, both momentous and tragic. Here popes are introduced to the world, here they are crowned, here they lie in state. (And here too, our beloved pontiff, Pope John Paul II, while conducting his weekly audience was wounded by a madman, just the day before this manuscript was accepted by the publisher. Just three weeks before that awful episode in Papal History, the author had stood practically on the same spot, exchanging waves and smiles with the Holy Father as he rode slowly through the admiring throng of his sons and daughters on the *Popemobile.)*

BASILICA SAN PIETRO

The largest church in Christendom, St. Peter's Basilica never fails to inspire, to thrill, to awe the visitor on his first or even on his hundredth visit.

With its massive travertine facade by Maderno, its Michelangelesque dome, its ten story-high baldacchino enhancing the Papal Altar, St. Peter's is actually the world's most stupendous tombstone, marking, and ennobling, the site of the burial of Christ's first Vicar on Earth. One hundred and eighty-six meters in length (with its magnificient atrium it comes to a total length of two hundred and twelve meters), St. Peter's is also a veritable repository of Renaissance and Baroque art, the major attraction among which is Michelangelo's Pietà (in the right side chapel as you enter the great hall).

Commissioned by the fiery Pope Julius II, the basilica is still referred to by many Romans as "The new St. Peter's" for it replaced the Constantinian edifice that stood on the same site for a thousand years.

Dwarfing the most famous cathedrals of the world— Notre Dame in Paris, St. Vitus in Prague, St. Paul's in London, Santa Maria del Fiore in Florence, St. Patrick's in New York—the basilica honoring the Prince of the Apostles can accommodate at one time eighty thousand worshipers.

THE APOSTOLIC PALACE

Rising behind the right arm of Bernini's colonnade is the *Palazzo Apostolico* with its Renaissance design, its high ceilings, its long corridors, its splendid marble staircases. The palace is, in fact, a conglomeration of edifices built mostly during the fifteenth and sixteenth centuries around a series of courtyards, but parts of it can be traced back as far as the fourth century.

The main palace was initiated under Nicholas III in the late thirteenth century and under subsequent popes it evolved into the sprawling, labyrinthine structure we see today. Of its more than 1400 rooms perhaps the most notable are the Clementine Hall, the Hall of the Consistory, and the Hall of the Congregations. In these halls the Holy Father will sometimes grant semi-private audiences to small pilgrimage groups.

On the top floor the Pope has his rather modest three-room apartment with its perfect view of St. Peter's Square. Downstairs on the second floor can be found the offices of the Secretariat of State which overlook the impressive courtyard of San Damaso.

Occupying a substantial part of the palace complex are the Vatican Museums, reached by a separate museum entrance.

THE VATICAN MUSEUMS

Housing perhaps the finest collection of ancient, classical, and Renaissance art, the Vatican Museums are reached by going through the right arm of the colonnade out onto Via Porta Angelica, past the Gate of Saint Anne, following the walls through Piazza del Risorgimento to the stately entrance commissioned by Pius XI on Viale Vaticano.

While the popes have for many centuries been avid patrons of the arts, it was not until Clement XIV (1769-1774) that the first papal museum was opened. But this was soon followed by another museum under Pius VI (1775-1799). Thus the oldest section of today's museum complex is called the *Museo Pio-Clementino*.

From 1800-1823 Pius VII enlarged the museum and the new addition received the name *Museo Chiaramonti* (Pius' family name). In these museums are gathered, by the hundreds, busts, statues, portraits from imperial times. Of particular interest is the Hall of Statues and the Hall of Busts (with contemporary portrayals of the likes of Caracalla, Octavian, Julius Caesar).

Devotees of the classical world thrill especially to the ancient carvings of Jupiter Enthroned and Laocoon and his sons. In the Chiaramonti wing also are found, in abundance, Greek sculptures, urns, sarcophagi, altars. Nearby is the *Museo Egizio* with its assortment of sixth century B.C. mummy cases and Egyptian urns, amphorae, and statues. This wing, established in 1836 by Pope Gregory XVI also contains a *Museo Etrusco* with archeological finds from southern Tuscany.

On one's trek through the vast museum one also passes along the Corridor of Tapestries, works of art—in thread—by Raphael and his students, portraying milestones in the life of Christ. Throughout the tour the visitor is treated to delightful views, through ceiling-to-floor windows, of the sprawling Vatican gardens, about which we will have a little more to say in due course.

THE SISTINE CHAPEL

Every tour of the Vatican Museums culminates with a stop in the Sistine Chapel, construction of which was ordered by Sixtus IV (hence its name) in 1473 to serve as the Pope's private chapel. Measuring forty meters in length, thirteen in width, and twenty in height, the Sistine is divided into two unequal parts by a unique marble screen, the work of Mino da Fiesole, and is graced with a cosmatesque pavement of the type so popular in early Christian Rome.

But it was under Julius II that the chapel acquired its artistic beauty when the "warrior pope" commissioned Michelangelo to fresco its vaults. Toiling backbreakingly for four years (1508-1512) on the scaffolding he himself built, the temperamental Tuscan artist covered the ceiling with highlights from Genesis. Here we see the fiery-eyed, white-maned, white-bearded Almighty in a fever of activity, in one panel separating the light from the darkness, in another, the land from the waters. In other panels also charged with divine energy and asplash with color, God is seen creating the sun and the moon—the two great lamps that will illuminate the earth, the first by day, the latter by night—and man and woman. The painted drama continues with the tragic fall of Adam and Eve and their expulsion from Paradise, with Noah's sacrifice and the awful deluge. Flanking these panels are enthroned prophets such as Jeremiah and the Sybil of Cumae. High up on the side walls of the chapel are frescoes by other Renaissance giants: Botticelli, Signorelli, Ghirlandaio, Perugino *et alii,* which feature scenes from the lives of Moses and Christ.

Three decades after he completed the ceiling, Michelangelo was summoned back to the Vatican by Paul III to paint the wall behind the altar. (By this time the artist was over sixty years of age and convinced that his time was running out. Almost another three decades later he was still putting in eighteen hour days.) Across two hundred square meters Michelangelo depicted the Last Judgment, at the center of which Christ is seen condemning the wicked amid much tumult and hysteria while trumpeters blast the terrible deafening music that will announce the end of the world. Surrounding Christ, isolating Him from the bedlam, are the Blessed Mother, John the Baptist, Andrew, Peter with the Keys, Paul, Simon of Cyrene, St. Sebastian, St. Catherine, the holy women of Jerusalem, Dismas the good thief, and other heirs of the Kingdom of Heaven. One leaves this place emotionally drained but spiritually elevated, perhaps musing that this is indeed a most unusual polling station. (For as pointed out earlier in the book, the Sistine Chapel is where the cardinals assemble to cast their ballots for a new pontiff.)

It should also be noted at this point that a lesser-known Vatican chapel, the *Cappella Paolina* built by Paul III, was also affrescoed by Michelangelo.

THE VATICAN LIBRARY

One of the most prestigious libraries in the world, the *Biblioteca Vaticana* has roots as far back as the fourth century and beyond. Since the very beginning of Christianity, popes have been in the habit of collecting documents, incunabula, books, and any other materials that aid and foster scholarship. The idea of a formal, extensive, and accessible Apostolic Vatican library, however, is usually credited to Nicholas V (1447-1455), one of the great Renaissance pontiffs. Sixtus IV (1471-1484) augmented the impressive collection of Nicholas and had the rooms housing it richly decorated by distinguished artists of the day, such as Ghirlandaio, Michelangelo's mentor. The main wing of the library was erected under orders of Sixtus V (1585-1590) and consisted of a long gallery, a vast hall with frescoes of Imperial Rome, and numerous smaller chambers where scholars might carry out their research. Four centuries later, under the direction of Pope Pius XI, a distinguished scholar and librarian himself (who, as Cardinal Achille Ratti, had been the prefect of the renowned Biblioteca Ambrosiana in Milan and later prefect of the Vatican Library), experts from the Library of Congress in Washington came to the Vatican and equipped the pontifical collection with a modern cataloguing system and more than seven miles of steel shelving. At this time also a new ventilating system was installed to preserve the precious documents by keeping the air from becoming either too moist or too dry.

Displayed in glass cases in the Sistine Hall of the library are precious manuscripts from as far back as the fourth century among which are the *"Codice Vaticano B"* of the Bible, the famous *"Codice Palinsesto"* with a first-century copy of Cicero's "De Republica," and the original manuscript of the "Canzoniae" by Petrarch.

In its entirety, the library consists of over 700,000 printed volumes, 60,000 codices, 7,000 incunabula and a museum division with artifacts from across the ages. These are accessible only to scholars who have been cleared by the Holy See. The greatest stillness I have ever experienced was in the reading hall where researchers sit at tables, which run the length of the room lined from floor to ceiling with books, and are served the volumes they need by whispering attendants.

The chief Vatican librarian is a cardinal and bears a most imposing title: "Librarian and Archivist of the Holy Roman Church."

In the archive section of the library can be found such intriguing documents as the transcript of Galileo's trial, the Concordat forged by Napoleon and Pius VII, the petition of Henry VIII to the Pope seeking an annulment of the King's marriage to Catherine of Aragon.

THE ROOMS OF RAPHAEL

Situated above the infamous and richly ornamented Borgia apartment, residence of Pope Alexander VI Borgia (1492-1503), are the *stanze* or rooms of Raphael. In

1500, the young master from Urbino was asked by Julius II to decorate the new pontifical quarters with frescoes. For the next dozen years, until his death on Good Friday in the year 1520, Raphael labored with some of his most promising students on this assignment. Some of the more spectacular results show the great fire in the borgo quarter of Rome during the reign of Leo IV (847-855). As the flames threaten even the venerable edifice of St. Peter's, the Holy Father is seen calmly imparting his benediction from a window of his palace and extinguishing the conflagration with the Sign of the Cross. Another masterpiece of the *stanze* is the School of Athens depicting the triumph of philosophy over ignorance. The scene is a vast hall with the greatest thinkers of antiquity coming and going, engaged animatedly in conversation. We see Plato and Aristotle emerging from the hall talking together; we see on the steps out front, the lonely, contemplative figure of Raphael's personal hero, and rival, Michelangelo.

PINACOTECA VATICANA

Rising majestically in the midst of the Vatican Gardens is the pink brick *Pinacoteca* (or art gallery), an imposing palace executed in the Lombard-Renaissance style by architect Luca Beltamini on commission of Pius XI.

Usually the last stop on a tour of the Vatican museum complex, the Pinacoteca boasts of a collection of paintings from the Byzantine era to the present day. Among this author's favorites are Giovanni Bonsi's "Madonna and Child" (fourteenth century), Margaritone d'Arezzo's St. Francis (twelfth century), and Giotto's "Christ Enthroned." Works by Fra Angelico, Fra Lippi, Perugino, Pinturicchio, Raphael, da Vinci, Titian, and Veronese are also featured here along with the creations of the Flemish, French, Dutch, and German masters.

THE VATICAN GARDENS

Originating in the middle ages, the lush Vatican Gardens ramble for fifty acres over the north and west slopes of Vatican Hill and afford the Pontiff a tranquil, verdant setting where each day he can "restoreth the soul" from the rigors of his awesome task. Here midst the countless fountains, ilexes, pines, shady recesses, and boxwood inglenooks, the Holy Father can meditate and contemplate and simply unwind, with only the eyes of an occasional imperial-age statue upon him.

With their marble or terracotta urns and occasional slender corinthian or ionic column protruding from the dense foliage and their ubiquitous watery music from the various fountains, the gardens bring the visitor back to the days of Maecenas when every patrician worth his salt had such a retreat.

Among the better known structures that rise out of the gardens is the *Casina* of Pius IV. This little Baroque gem with its harmonious proportions and delicate structure was the work of Pirro Ligorio, and served Pius (1558-1562) as his summer villa. The intellectual pontiff fostered learning throughout his reign and hosted meetings of the leading minds of the day at his *casina*. These sessions, called *Notti Vaticanae* (Vatican Evenings), revolved around discussions of poetry, philosophy, and sacred subjects. Later popes granted audiences in the charming courtyard of the casina, and the building now serves as the seat of the Pontifical Academy of Sciences.

From any point in the gardens the visitor is afforded matchless views of the great dome and endless vignettes, splashed with bright colors from flower and rock gardens and silver mists from fountain jets, to photograph. Various other buildings rise haphazardly out of the gardens. There is for one the Ethiopian College, a seminary for producing future African bishops; for another, the Teutonic College which specializes in archeological studies, a field in which the Vatican has long taken an active and enthusiastic interest. Also punctuating the gardens are portions of the original ninth-century Vatican wall by Leo IV and a few of its watchtowers. One of these, the tower of St. John, was refurbished as a modest Papal summer retreat under the direction of Pope John XXIII who disliked the forty minute drive to Castel Gandolfo. This unique apartment with its idyllic views of the surrounding gardens was used by Patriarch Athenagoras of Constantinople during his ecumenical call on Paul VI in the summer of 1969. Here, too, rested the long-suffering Cardinal Mindszenty of Hungary during his visit to the Holy See in 1971.

For this writer the most dramatic point in the gardens is on the southernmost periphery where stands, on a gentle knoll, a statue of St. Peter, clutching the keys and staring incredulously at the colossal church in his honor.

THE CITIZENRY

The proudest boast of the ancient world was *"Civis Romanus sum."* (I am a Roman citizen.) Today many an Italian would be delighted to be able to say *"sono cittadino del Vaticano."* (I am a citizen of the Vatican.) For the Vaticanite lives in a serene and fascinating land where there is no crime, no customs, no taxes, no military duty; where the rents are low and the general cost of living far lower than it is just beyond the walls. There are no workers' unions, hence no strikes to worry over. There is no blight, no run-down area, no district where it is unsafe to walk, even at midnight. In this unique land, where citizenship is obtained only by birth or appointment, men outnumber women by about nine to one. The women are usually the wives of firemen, cooks, gardeners, elevator operators, laborers, pharmacists, chauffeurs, clerks, and the colorful band of maintenance men called *Sanpietrini* who are responsible for the care of St. Peter's Basilica.

The administrative office which oversees the maintenance of the basilica and the work of the *San-*

pietrini has the rather charming name of *La Reverenda Fabbrica di San Pietro.* (The Reverend Structure of Saint Peter's.)

Among the citizens of the Vatican are also to be found a few cardinals (and their aides), nuns who operate the religious article shops, the bookstore, the kitchens in the Apostolic Palace, and the seminarians studying at the Ethiopian College along with their instructors.

There is no school system in the Vatican. Therefore the children fortunate enough to grow up in this historic and artistic setting must receive their education in the schools of Rome. After school hours these kids can be seen roughhousing in the Holy Father's gardens, running errands for a little *mancia* (tip), playing volleyball and basketball with the cassock-clad African seminarians.

There is also no mass-transit system in the Vatican. Transportation is simply not necessary in a country that can be covered on foot from border to border in a matter of minutes. To take a train or a bus to any other point in Italy or in Europe, the Vatican citizen must go into Rome.

THE STREETS

Within the ancient fortifications of tiny Vatican City there are more than thirty slender, cobblestoned streets and squares. Downtown Vatican, or the business district you might call it, lies to the far right of Piazza San Pietro and is reached through the Porta Sant'Anna, the Vatican's service entrance on the Borgo Angelicum. Just after entering through this gate, one sees, on the right, the Church of St. Anne. This narrow and busy thoroughfare, the Via Sant'Anna, leads past the grocery store, or the *Annona* as it is known to Vatican insiders, the post office, the car pool and garage, the bookstore, and the offices of *L'Osservatore Romano*. There are three intersections along St. Anne's Street: the Street of the Pilgrim, the Street of Typography, and the Street of

Posts. Off of these side streets run a number of tiny back alleys, grandiosely called streets also. There is no residential section as such. Apartment buildings here and there mingle with the edifices of the Vatican bureaucracy.

THE COURTYARDS

Too small for genuine piazzas like *Navona* and *del Popolo* in Rome, the Vatican contents itself with the airiness of its courtyards, prominent among which are the *Belvedere* with its impressive centerpiece fountain, the *San Damaso* overlooked by the huge gallery of thirteen arcades known as the *Logge di Raffaello,* since they are decorated with scriptural scenes by the genius of Urbino, and the *Pigna,* dominated at one end by an enormous bronze pine cone set in a splendid apse. This remnant of old Rome was once a fountain that oozed water through its many pores. Pius XII occasionally used the Belvedere for audiences, and Pope John XXIII, his successor, often reminisced how, as a seminarian and young priest in Rome, he used to love to attend Pius X's audiences in the court of San Damaso.

THE CHURCHES

Since the Vatican, a golf-course-sized country, contains St. Peter's Basilica, the world's largest church, one would think it unnecessary for the residents to have other houses of worship. But they do. In fact, St. Peter's, as grand as it is, does not enjoy the distinction of the Vatican's parish church. That claim goes to the Church of Sant'Anna at the gate by the same name. And in addition to St. Anne's there are the Church of St. Pellegrino (the oldest house of worship in Vatican City), the Church of St. Stephen of the Abyssinians, the Church of St. Martin of the Swiss (actually the chapel for the Swiss Guards), the Church of St. Sebastian (for the Vatican gendarmes), and the Church of Santa Maria in Camposanto, also known as the "Teutonic Church" since it is used by the German personnel assigned to the Vatican.

THE CEMETERIES

Camposanto means cemetery and the Vatican has four of these. To the left, after entering the enclave through the Gate of the Bells, is the Teutonic Cemetery. Old, small, and rarely used nowadays, this burial ground is, as suggested by its name, for the German element of the Vatican populace. Originally for German pilgrims who happened to die while in Rome, the Teutonic will see activity today only when a German prelate or worker in the Curia expresses a wish to be interred there.

Another ancient *camposanto* but no longer used at all is the little one in the courtyard of *L'Osservatore Romano*. There is a third in the grottoes beneath St. Anne's church and a fourth—for use by the Swiss Guard—behind the Church of St. Pellegrino.

VATICAN RADIO

Over the entrance to the Vatican's broadcasting center there is a Latin inscription which translates loosely to: "So that the Voice of the Supreme Pontiff may be heard for the glory of Christ and the salvation of souls in all corners of the globe."

Designed by Marconi, who was brought in by Pius XI, and supervised by him until his death in 1937, Vatican Radio is operated by the Jesuit order. Modernization of the facility is an on-going process. Each broadcast begins with the words *Laudetur Jesus Christus*. Praised be Jesus Christ.

With its twin transmitting towers, looking rather like incongruous steel sculptures in a Renaissance ambience, Vatican Radio became an information center regarding refugees during World War II. The station would transmit short wave messages to Vatican agents around the world who were engaged in refugee assistance programs.

Station identification every half hour or so takes the form of the hymn *Christus Vincit* or the great bells of

St. Peter's. There are daily broadcasts in dozens of languages. Speeches of the Pope at his weekly audiences, along with his *Urbi et Orbi* blessings on special occasions, are standard fare of Vatican Radio.

The facilities can also be employed as a telegraph system to send messages from the Secretariat of State to its diplomats stationed around the world.

Broadcasting for twenty hours a day, Vatican Radio likes to present educational programs on the role of the Church in the modern world.

L'OSSERVATORE ROMANO

The Vatican has a semi-official newspaper, *L'Osservatore Romano* where Latin and Italian are printed side by side. Sharing printing facilities with the journal is the publishing house of the Polyglot Press which, as the name indicates, publishes in a host of languages. In fact the Polyglot Press has fonts of types of every major language of today's world.

Pronouncements of the Holy See are reported in Latin, still the official language of the Roman Church—with accompanying Italian translations. Founded in 1861, the *Osservatore* also reports political news from around the world and editorializes on the key issues of our time—social, cultural, economic. Papal speeches and encyclicals along with news concerning the Holy See can be found on the front page. The *Osservatore* also publishes an illustrated weekly each Sunday, *L'Osservatore della Domenica* and a more ambitious monthly, *Ecclesia.*

The newspaper is also held in esteem for having the fewest typographical or factual errors of any daily in the world.

LATIN

Though the vernacular Mass has considerably reduced the role of the ancient tongue, the venerable language of old Rome is still maintained as the official language of the Holy See. While Italian is the working day-to-day language of the Curia and the Vatican bureaucracy, and while in its correspondence with other nations the Holy See endeavors to use the appropriate modern language, Latin is still employed in communication with smaller countries using little-known tongues and is also used in granting rescripts and in publishing papal encyclicals, and bulls, and other official documents. Pontifical ceremonies are still conducted in the venerable tongue, and it is always a thrill for this writer to stand in the basilica or the square and recite or sing with fellow Catholics from every nation on every continent, in the company of His Holiness, the *Gloria* or the *Credo* or the *Sanctus*. Nothing else impresses upon me more the true universality of the Church, and I for one would like to see the once extensive role of Latin reinstated in Church ritual for that very reason. John Paul II has on several occasions expressed the same wish.

THE MOSAIC STUDIO

Connected to the office of *La Reverenda Fabbrica di San Pietro* is the Vatican's Mosaic Studio which came into existence in the late seventeenth century upon the need to replace many of the canvas paintings in Saint Peter's. The mosaics which ornament the interior of the cupola were composed in this little factory, a visit to which is a memorable experience and a compelling lesson in concentration and patience. As little boys living in Rome, my sons never tired of stopping at the studio to watch the artists absorbed in their work and painstakingly selecting with slender tweezers one tiny tile after another from a stock of some 30,000 different tints, sometimes searching for just the right item for what seemed like a mini-eternity. (But then everything about the Vatican seems to speak of eternity.)

Mosaic works are executed here for churches throughout Rome, Italy, and Europe. You may be surprised to learn that you too may place an order for a small mosaic copy of a favorite religious picture.

THE VATICAN RAILROAD

Vatican City has a few yards of track that are actually a spur of the Italian railway system and were installed just after the signing of the Lateran Treaty to afford the Pontiff the means to travel direct from his miniature land to all parts of the Italian peninsula and the European continent. Yet no Pontiff ever availed himself of the facility. The station, built of travertine marble from nearby Tivoli, looks rather like a bank and is most peculiar in that it has no ticket-booths, no newsstands, no coffee-bars, no electronic board listing arrivals and departures. What it does have, however, are religious sculptures symbolizing travel. There is one of Christ on the Sea of Galilee, another of Elias rising to Heaven. A true "Iron Curtain"—two massive cast iron gates that draw back and disappear like the doors of an elevator and are electronically operated—seals off the Vatican spur from Rome's tracks just beyond the walls. Now and then the gates part to allow in a load of freight. Another peculiarity of the Vatican Railway is that there are no personnel. There is, though, a stationmaster.

THE GOVERNORATE

While the Pope is the constitutional head of Vatican City State with full legislative, executive, and judicial powers, the fact is that he and his curia occupy themselves principally with matters of the Holy See. Affairs of state are in practice largely the province of the Vatican Governorate, made up of numerous departments such as the Post Office, the General Accounting Office, the Legal Department. Vatican Radio and the Vatican Observatory are also under the management of *Il Governorato*. The offices of the Governorate are housed in a splendid, yellow brick palace directly behind the Basilica.

VATICAN FINANCES

Vatican City State and the Holy See have five main sources of revenue. One is Peter's Pence, a collection taken up once a year in churches throughout the world. The voluntary contributions of the faithful to this fund go toward the maintenance of the Holy City. A second source is the largesse of wealthy devout Catholics around the globe who across the centuries have seen fit to stipulate in their wills that upon their death the Church of Rome shall be the sole heir of their possessions. The Lateran Financial Convention, signed in 1929 when the Vatican became a state, provides a third source of income. At that time the new state received, in compensation from the Italian government for confiscation in 1870 of the Papal territory throughout central Italy, $40,000,000 in cash and $52,000,000 in 5% Italian bonds. A fourth avenue for funds for the Pope's state are the various investments made by the Vatican with the capital from the third source. This rather large portion of Vatican revenue is used to administer the world-wide charitable and missionary work of Mother Church and to keep her priests and nuns alive in communist countries where their properties have been confiscated. The entrance fees of the Vatican Museum and the business transacted in the mosaic studio and post office provide a fifth source.

While the Vatican does enjoy a vast artistic and architectural wealth, this does not translate into real, spendable money. It helps only to attract, perennially, millions of visitors through the turnstiles. The living quarters and office facilities of the modern Vatican are a study in Spartan simplicity and even in austerity. Long gone is the day of the Renaissance cardinal hosting lavish dinner parties in the palatial splendor of his townhouse or country villa.

The Vatican's gold reserves are on deposit with the Federal Reserve Bank of New York. Recent pontiffs have scrupulously refused to involve themselves personally with Vatican finances, choosing to leave such matters in the hands of a special council of fiscal experts.

The Vatican Bank serves as a clearing house for the numerous financial transactions of the state.

It might be noted that North America, i.e., the United States and Canada, is the biggest contributor to Peter's Pence, for the Church in this corner of the world is prosperous and free while in many other areas it is impoverished, and in some others, both impoverished and suppressed. The Church seems to find its strength, economically at least, in genuine democracies where religious freedom is a reality, not merely a cliché.

THE SWISS GUARD

No soldier anywhere in the world has a uniform so resplendent nor an assignment so cherished as that of any member of the Swiss Guard, this little state's little army. Founded by the "Warrior Pope," Julius II, in 1505, the Guard is colorfully clad in puffy-sleeved outfits striped blue, gold, and red that look like something out of a German operetta. Unarmed except for ceremonial halberds and swords, the troops stand guard at all of the border checkpoints—the Gate of the Bells, the Bronze Door, the Gate of St. Anne, the Gate of the Holy Office—snapping salutes to prelates coming and going, and protect the Pope at his public appearances, lending additional splendor and panoply to all pontifical ceremonies.

An admirer of the Swiss military for many years earlier, Pope Julius II asked the Swiss government for 200 of its finest troops to help defend the then beleaguered Papal States. On January 27, 1506, the Swiss Guard marched into Rome for the first time and has never left.

On May 6, 1527, the Vatican was stormed by allied Spanish and German forces. When the dust settled, the valiant Swiss had lost 147 men. (But the enemy's toll exceeded 1,000.) In the meantime, Pope Clement VII and his curia, under escort by the remaining Swiss troops, reached the fortress of Castel Sant'Angelo a half mile away on the banks of the Tiber and lived to tell about their heart-pounding flight to safety.

Today the Guard numbers but 90 men who are drawn from the French and German cantons of Switzerland. To qualify, a candidate must be of Swiss citizenship, a practicing Catholic, and a bachelor under 25 years of age. He must also have completed his term of military service in his homeland. He must stand at least five-foot-eight inches tall and be of excellent character.

The normal hitch is two years, with options for re-enlistment. Many do stay on for more than one tour of duty and some make the Guard their career.

The Swiss Guard has its own barracks, its own chaplain, and—as mentioned earlier—its own chapel. There is also a canteen for after-hours billiards, cards, darts, and even a few brews.

Easily the most photographed soldiers in the world—tourists snap their cameras furiously at the mere sight of a member of the Pope's army—these lucky young men are required to take courses in Italian and trade and commercial subjects to prepare them for post-Vatican careers. They receive a salary of approximately four hundred dollars a month, seventy-five of which is given back for board.

The present commander of the Guard is Commandante Franz Pfyffer von Altishofen.

PONTIFICAL INSTITUTES

Throughout the city of Rome can be found a number of Pontifical institutes for theological and ecclesiastical studies. Preeminent among these institutes, which are under the direct supervision of the Holy See, are the Jesuit-staffed Pontifical Gregorian University, known affectionately by the seminarians and priests matriculating there simply as "The Greg," the Lateran University with its faculty drawn from the clergy of Rome, and the Pontifical Urban University.

Conclusion

So then, we have been to the Vatican, that wonderful and most unique little country just up the hill from the Tiber, a country encircled by soaring medieval walls and surrounded by a foreign city, a country where there is no taxation, no privation, no crime, no unrest, no unemployment.

We have traced its origin, its evolution, its role in the modern world. We have examined its system of government, met its head of state, descended into its subterranean extraterritorial holdings.

The Vatican. A country whose postal service is prompt and efficient, whose jail cells are always empty, whose national revenues are used principally for foreign aid, whose legislation is concerned chiefly with the salvation of souls, whose pace of life is refreshingly tranquil and slow.

Here there is no Department of Defense, no War Department, no arms race. For this miniature state is consecrated to the message of the Prince of Peace.

In fact, its 90 man army reminds one not of war at all but of a dreamy watercolor. Though officially charged with the protection of the Holy See, the Swiss Guards are, in our times, largely ceremonial, directing traffic, manning the gates of this fascinating enclave. (Another Vatican claim to uniqueness is that it is probably the only country on earth without a single traffic light.)

And the head of State is the very terrestrial vicar of the most celebrated Peacemaker of all time, Jesus Christ. Just last spring I stood in the square with 300,000 others to hear the 60-year old Pontiff, John Paul II, deliver his

Easter message, "to the city and to the world," the theme of which was "peace." Dressed in white and gold vestments and episcopal miter, His Holiness stepped out on the 17th century balcony of St. Peter's and under a cloudless sky proclaimed: "To the Church and the world I send a fervent and cordial greeting of peace, of Easter peace, of true and lasting peace. I direct these greetings to all those who live in anxiety, in tension, under threat; to individuals and peoples—in particular to those who have the greatest need of peace. *Pax vobiscum!"*

(Ironically, this same apostle of peace, just three weeks later, would himself be the victim of a senseless, purposeless, unspeakable act of violence in the same square, just a hundred yards or so from the spot where the first Roman Pontiff gave his life for Mother Church.)

This land, whose entire territory, practically speaking, is taken up by a biscuit-colored palace, an outsized Baroque church, and a sprawling garden, could be the one last hope of humankind. In the final analysis, if civilization is to survive, above the daily polemical utterances of the leaders of other geographically larger nations must be heard and heeded the gentle, fervent, and eternal plea of the head of State of Vatican City: "No more war! War never again!"

This is the Vatican, a country whose most sacred shrine is not the tomb of some fearless native warrior but the humble grave of a shy and awkward fisherman from a distant land; a country which is nothing more nor less than one rather sizeable monument to the mentor of that fisherman; a country which beckons all people everywhere to come and feel its long and Apostolic heritage, to enjoy its treasures of art and architecture, to celebrate the Sacred Mysteries with its Pontiff, to share in its solemn mission to bring peace to our troubled planet.

And from here let us go out upon the highways and byways of the world to spread the good news coming daily out of the Vatican: *"Christus surrexit!"*

INDEX

-About the Author-

Frank J. Korn is the author of *Rome—The Enchanted City,* a documentary of the Italian capital and a personal memoir of Korn's days there as a Fulbright Scholar back in the 60's, and *From Peter to John Paul II,* a warmly written history of the Chair of Peter. He is currently at work on a novel set in Rome during World War II, and on a study of the American Presidency. A professor of English, Latin and Italian, Korn is also a feature writer for numerous magazines and newspapers. He also lectures on Christian Rome and Roman Archeology. Since his Fulbright days, Korn and his wife Camille and their three sons, Frank, Ronald and John, have been part-time Romans, spending summers, Easter seasons, and other recesses from school in the Eternal City. The rest of the year they call Kenilworth, New Jersey their hometown.

Daughters of St. Paul

IN MASSACHUSETTS
   50 St. Paul's Ave., Jamaica Plain, Boston, MA 02130;
      617-522-8911; 617-522-0875
   172 Tremont Street, Boston, MA 02111; **617-426-5464;**
      617-426-4230
IN NEW YORK
   78 Fort Place, Staten Island, NY 10301; **212-447-5071**
   59 East 43rd Street, New York, NY 10017; **212-986-7580**
   625 East 187th Street, Bronx, NY 10458; **212-584-0440**
   525 Main Street, Buffalo, NY 14203; **716-847-6044**
IN NEW JERSEY
   Hudson Mall — Route 440 and Communipaw Ave.,
      Jersey City, NJ 07304; **201-433-7740**
IN CONNECTICUT
   202 Fairfield Ave., Bridgeport, CT 06604; **203-335-9913**
IN OHIO
   2105 Ontario St. (at Prospect Ave.), Cleveland, OH 44115; **216-621-9427**
   25 E. Eighth Street, Cincinnati, OH 45202; **513-721-4838**
IN PENNSYLVANIA
   1719 Chestnut Street, Philadelphia, PA 19103; **215-568-2638**
IN VIRGINIA
   1025 King St., Alexandria, VA 22314
IN FLORIDA
   2700 Biscayne Blvd., Miami, FL 33137; **305-573-1618**
IN LOUISIANA
   4403 Veterans Memorial Blvd., Metairie, LA 70002; **504-887-7631,**
      504-887-0113
   1800 South Acadian Thruway, P.O. Box 2028, Baton Rouge, LA 7082.
      504-343-4057; 504-343-3814
IN MISSOURI
   1001 Pine Street (at North 10th), St. Louis, MO 63101; **314-621-0346;**
      314-231-1034
IN ILLINOIS
   172 North Michigan Ave., Chicago, IL 60601; **312-346-4228**
      312-346-3240
IN TEXAS
   114 Main Plaza, San Antonio, TX 78205; **512-224-8101**
IN CALIFORNIA
   1570 Fifth Avenue, San Diego, CA 92101; **714-232-1442**
   46 Geary Street, San Francisco, CA 94108; **415-781-5180**
IN HAWAII
   1143 Bishop Street, Honolulu, HI 96813; **808-521-2731**
IN ALASKA
   750 West 5th Avenue, Anchorage AK 99501; **907-272-8183**
IN CANADA
   3022 Dufferin Street, Toronto 395, Ontario, Canada
IN ENGLAND
   128, Notting Hill Gate, London W11 3QG, England
   133 Corporation Street, Birmingham B4 6PH, England
   5A-7 Royal Exchange Square, Glasgow G1 3AH, England
   82 Bold Street, Liverpool L1 4HR, England
IN AUSTRALIA
   58 Abbotsford Rd., Homebush, N.S.W., Sydney 2140, Australia

DATE DUE

6/05			

IDEAL 3370 UNGUMMED, 3371 GUMMED   PRINTED IN U.S.A.